PRAISE FOR
PUNCH BACK

"How you respond when you're at your lowest determines if you'll emerge as a victor or victim. In Punch Back, Scott and Kristi's story will infuse you with strength to stay in the fight, no matter what life throws at you!"

John Bevere
Best-selling Author & Minister
Co-founder of Messenger International & MessengerX

"Run as fast as you can to pick up a copy of this outstanding book by my friends Kristi and Scott Schatzline! This outstanding effort perfectly captures the obstacles they've overcome as they continue to demonstrate a strong personal witness for our Lord and Savior Jesus Christ, while understanding that it is only through Him that we are able to succeed and move forward!"

John H. Merrill
Secretary of State, Alabama

"I've always defined adversity as an unwanted outcome. How you handle that departure from the vision you had is everything. Scott and Kristi Schatzline have created a riveting book that shows you how to rise up when you've been knocked down. Incredibly written and overflowing with inspiring stories, you will find a new outlook on life in the pages ahead. If you want to learn to punch back when life knocks the shout out of you, this is a must read."

Coach Micheal Burt
17X Author and America's Coach

"Punch Back *is a real triumph! Each sentence is captivating and compels the reader to engage with Scott and Kristi's living testimony. Their authenticity and masterfully worded details will certainly be life-altering for each reader. The interweaving of their childhood stories, their adult family's recent events, the catastrophic incidents, and the healing journey of Kristi's heroic grit melded with Scott's tenacity provide a canvas with vibrant strokes of color. This storytelling technique provides depth to the entire masterpiece."*

Al & Tava Brice
Founding Pastors, Covenant Love Church

"We were privileged to know Scott and Kristi before they ever had to step into the fight of their lives. We knew them to be champions. Now, to watch them fight back with such resilience and faith, not backing down or quitting during this season, has increased our respect for the warriors they truly are. They found themselves in a do-or-die situation and exemplified greatness. All who know them are better for it, as they make a daily decision to choose life."

Steve & Mary Alessi
Pastors, Metro Life Church

"Pastors Scott and Kristi Schatzline are overcomers! Their story is an inspiration to all who know them. Back from the dead, Pastor Scott truly is a dead man walking. Pastor Kristi is a warrior like no other for her man and their destiny. Both Scott and Kristi are heroes of faith, and had the Bible been written during our day, *they would have most likely made the cut of the Hebrews 11 Hall of Faith. By faith, Scott and Kristi continue to punch back the darkness and walk in His light. While you read* Punch Back, *get ready to be inspired to live another day, fight harder, survive, and ultimately, thrive in this journey we call life."*

Harry & Cheryl Salem
Salem Family Ministries and Miss America 1980

"No matter what life throws at us, we each have the same decision: succumb to circumstance or punch back and fight. In this book, Pastors Scott and Kristi Schatzline share their near-death experience so you can punch back with faith, the power of community, fervent prayer, and daily commitment to live each day to its fullest. It is your time to punch back!"

Doug & Thea Wood
Bestselling Authors, Speakers, Entrepreneurs,
and Co-Founders of Valor Global Online

"I've known Scotty and Kristi Schatzline for a long time. I met Scott as a wee boy when I preached for his dad, Pat Sr. I watched his life unfold from youth ministry to music ministry and then to the senior pastor role at Daystar in Tuscaloosa, Alabama. Each step was marked by the anointing of the Holy Ghost. I remember when he met Kristi. They were perfect together. The church was growing, everything seemed perfect until . . .

We all have "until" moments. That is when you know if the anointing is on you—or in you. After that moment, the world stopped. For days we wondered if Scott would make it (I honestly wondered if Kristi would). Yet, their song, from deep inside, kept on singing. Faith like I've rarely seen was manifest in their walk. Scott has had to relearn everything! Kristi became Scott's lifeline. However, there was one thing Scott did not have to learn again: his love for Jesus. What was in him was stronger than what had happened to him.

In this remarkable book you will literally walk with Scott and Kristi through the "valley of the shadow of death" and discover what this remarkable couple has discovered: "thy rod and staff they comfort me." I promise you that after you read about their journey, you will never be the same again."

Philip Cameron
Missionary-Evangelist, Singer, and Author

"Man, the Schatzlines have the purest hearts! They are truly a blessing to know. Pastor Scott and Pastor Kristi are the epitome of love, strength, and faith. Their miraculous journey of life and trusting in God is a must read!"

Rashad and Chelsea Johnson
NFL Legend and Coach

"Many wonder what happens when the enemy not only knocks you down but attempts to take you out. Why does it feel like your faith has failed you when the ten count has been called and you're still laying on the mat? This is the story that few even have the opportunity to tell. Scott and Kristi's testimonies answer these questions and empower us to keep sweating, keep fighting, keep swinging, keep moving, keep faithing, and keep living! Their story is a complicated tapestry woven with moments of faith, fear, loneliness, hope, anger, triumph, and joy, but most of all, extravagant grace! Only the power of God could navigate them through. We are personal witnesses to the audacious faith that God has given our friends for this journey. If you too, have been counted out, let this story fuel you, and relish your faith life again."

Patrick and Christina Dopson
Associate Pastor, Oak Cliff Bible Fellowship, Dr. Tony Evans &
Billboard Gospel Artist & Songwriter

"*Punch Back is an incredible story of overcoming unimaginable tragedies and challenges. We have known the Schatzlines for years. We've seen their path to success, witnessed an unexpected and devastating tragedy, and watched them build back to become better than ever! It truly is miraculous. This story will leave you forever impacted and inspired. Everyone should read this book. It is life changing.*"

Coach Mario and Jessica Cristobal
Head Football Coach, Miami Hurricanes

"*Wow! Punch Back is a powerful and life altering book. Scott and Kristi take you on a miraculous journey from death to life. This book is not just a story of victory, but also a life book that dives deep into conquering the enemy. You will be stirred to go to another level in your faith. We have watched these two use their story to restore and revive lives of others. It is time for you to punch back!*"

Patrick and Karen Schatzline
Evangelists, Authors, & CEOs
Remnant Ministries International

"*Scott and Kristi have stood up to the ultimate challenge of death and have come out the other side with tremendous grit and perseverance. They are incredible human beings who have much to share on facing what life can throw at you. Enjoy this incredible book that will make you smile and cry but will also leave you better prepared to treat obstacles as the way.*"

Dr. Wayne Scott Andersen
New York Times Bestselling Author

PUNCH BACK

*A Miracle Story of Rising Up
When Life Knocks You Down*

SCOTT AND KRISTI SCHATZLINE

PUNCH BACK

Copyright © 2022 Scott and Kristi Schatzline

Published by

STORY ⫼ CHORUS

Learn more at StoryChorus.com

DEDICATION

We dedicate this book to the countless people who have walked with us through this journey. We would not have made it without so many fighting with us. While the list could be endless, we give Jesus, our first love, all the glory and honor. This book is dedicated to our parents, siblings, children, and friends who have stood by our side. And it is dedicated in honor to the mother of all mothers: Deborah Schatzline. You taught Scott how to love, worship, and preach. Your direction filled him with the Holy Spirit at seven years old changing his life forever. Like Jesus, Scott is proud to be a mama's boy! As you always said, we are "looking to the throne!" Our hope for everyone who reads this book is that God will invade your life and meet your needs. We encourage you to lean into this book and let God talk to you individually!

With all His love,
Scott and Kristi

CONTENTS

FOREWORD

*W*hat happened to our dad was terrifying. However, what has happened because of him and our mom is what we'd like to share with you.

This book is more than a story of ultimate tragedy narrowly avoided. It's an inspiration for anyone who has, or will, go through the darkest valley of their lives.

If there's ever been a constant in the Schatzline home, it is how our parents have given everything they had (and some-times more) to love, serve, and lead people well. As children, we can hardly remember a year without someone who needed a home staying with us. For them, loving people is like breathing—it happens everywhere they go.

However, the pages ahead share the story of the hardest season our family has ever faced. We endured trauma upon trauma, and disappointments that stretched like an endless mountain range. So as you read, please understand you are hearing from real people who suffered very real pain, yet found the strength to fight through every obstacle.

If you are hurting, you will find help here. Because that is what our parents do: help hurting people. You will also discover hope and inspiration, and understand that miracles still happen. We know, because our dad is proof.

More than anything, we want you to know how deeply we love, respect, and admire our parents. And as you read this book, we believe you will understand why.

With love,
Ethan, Noah, Keithan, Isaiah, and Destiny

A NOTE FOR READERS

We're thrilled to share our story with you. You'll get the whole picture in the rest of the book, but Scott and I (Kristi) wanted to give you a note about how we wrote it.

Our story is a collection of our memories and the perspective of our friends, family, Daystar Family Church team, and numerous medical professionals. It's mainly written from my perspective because I've had a front-row seat to Scott's painful, difficult, yet remarkable journey. But if you know Scott, he has a *lot* to say, as well!

My heart (Scott) for you is to believe that no matter what you're going through, God's not done with you. Everyone is fighting a battle we can't see. I don't care if you're the most successful entrepreneur or Coach Saban of the Alabama Crimson Tide, you're going through hard things. There is so much pain in this world, but I need you to promise me you won't give up.

I've learned that adversity introduces you to yourself—so there is great purpose in your pain! As my beautiful wife, Kristi Love (only I get to call her that!), and I open up about the good, bad, and ugly of our story to you, we'll always note who's talking by dropping our name in (parentheses) so you can keep things straight.

This is a different kind of book, but we've been living a different kind of life than we ever imagined. We are honored to have you along for the ride.

Now let's get started.

A DEAD MAN SPEAKS

Some days you make decisions that are big. Like obviously big. Do we buy the small house with the pool or the big one in the country? Do I go to the liberal arts school or play it safe at the state university? Do I marry this person or run far, far away? Other days, you make small, seemingly insignificant decisions that somehow change your life forever.

On July 4, 2020, that's exactly what happened to Jessica Gray Lee.

Jessica wasn't supposed to be working. It was supposed to be her day off. Her autoimmune symptoms were lighting up like a solar flare. And besides, who would watch her kids? Still, her manager begged and pleaded with her to come into the hospital for a shift. They desperately needed a speech therapist and Jessica was one of the best. She almost said no. She would've had every right to. But she pulled on her scrubs, pushed through the shooting pains, and showed up anyway, ready to help patients find their voices.

Hospitals have soundtracks all their own. Machines beep, buzz, and spout off the occasional scream for help. Those are the noises you expect. But when she stepped into her first patient's room, something was different.

Worship music, she noticed. Her tension eased as she was welcomed into the atmosphere filled with the Holy Spirit. She was grateful for it, because this patient was a serious case. A man lay in the hospital bed with his concerned, and very exhausted, wife pinned to his side. Jessica introduced herself and shared her role with them.

The wife explained his recent history. It was bad. He'd been in the intensive care unit (ICU), totally nonverbal just a week before. Jessica saw desperation and pain in her eyes–but there was hope, too. The wife held her husband's hand tightly. It was obvious she hadn't left his side and certainly didn't plan to. However, the damage seemed done–this man needed a miracle if he would ever speak again.

Jessica began her evaluation.

"What is this?" she asked the patient, holding a cup.

He mumbled, vaguely repeating back her words. So she tried again, and again, and again. Still nothing. But after a few turns of this, something changed. The energy in the room shifted and the man's gaze went from wide-eyed and blurry to laser focused, making intense eye contact.

He spoke. His voice was soft and raspy. But words that shouldn't have been possible poured out of him.

"You are powerfully anointed for something *big*. God loves your heart," the patient said. "Your husband is a very powerful man, and your children are anointed. Get ready, prepare, because *big* change is coming."

Tears streamed down her face. What she was experiencing was medically impossible. This man couldn't even identify a cup. His wife's hand floated to her mouth. She sat stunned, listening, watching, hoping.

He laid his hands on her forehead and shoulder, and said quietly, "God sees your hurt and wants to heal it in Jesus's name."

Jessica's small choice to work that day turned into a life-altering lesson: *when a man who was dead just two weeks ago prophecies over you, you listen.*

Those prophetic moments encouraged her deeply, but it did even more for us, because we were there, too. Scott was that voiceless man in the hospital bed. Kristi was that distraught wife wondering if she'd ever have her husband back. We were clinging to threads; this experience felt like we'd just grabbed ahold of a lifeline.

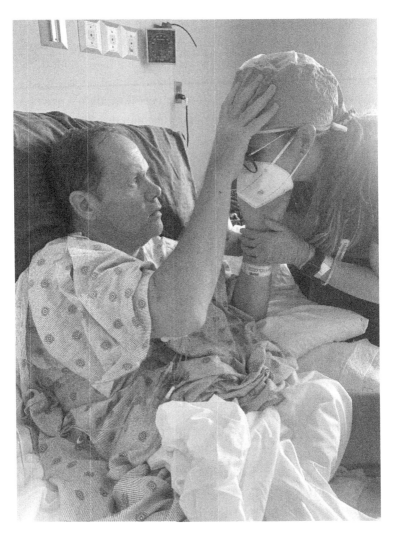

Jessica later shared that Scott's words breathed life back into her because she'd been stuck in a holding pattern. Waiting for God. Wondering if His words so many years ago would ever come true. Scott was on target, because he affirmed exactly that message.

In the waiting, disappointment, and seemingly endless preparation for *the next*, God used a man who couldn't even recognize a cup to call out hidden things in her heart.

Like Jessica, we have been waiting, too.

When will we get our lives back?

When will Scott be fully healed?

When will it all make sense?

When will our marriage be what it used to be?

When will this depression lift?

When will the tears dry?

When will God's promises over our lives be fulfilled?

Endless questions keep us company in the waiting. This book is both a story and an answer. The new story God is writing in our lives. It has been filled with bitter tears, lament, and hopelessness. But even more, it has shown us God's faithfulness to meet us there. He is doing a new thing. And it is our answer to what we have done in the waiting.

What does life look like in between promise and fulfillment? How do you navigate those gray waters? Where do you find life in a land of death? This book isn't about textbook Sunday school answers that fit nicely on a flannelgraph. It's about the authentic guts of losing everything and wondering if you'll ever get it back.

It's also about keeping your fighting spirit. It's Scott's miracle story of standing back up when life knocked us down. It's what the battle to *Punch Back* looked like every single day! When we wanted to throw in the towel or stay flat on the mat, we had to make the decision to keep fighting for what God had planned next.

If you are in the waiting, welcome to our story. We pray that, like Jessica's decision to pick up an extra shift, your small decision to pick up this book will blossom into life-changing hope. Hope that's battle-tested and strong enough to build a life on.

God has something to say to you. You will find your purpose, even in your pain. We trust God's faithfulness to us will help you see His fingerprints in your life, too.

All about the love,
Scott and Kristi

Chapter 1

WHEN LIFE STOPS

A *wife always knows when something is up with her husband.* It was Sunday morning, May 17, 2020, and I knew something was wrong with Scott. We are the pastors at Daystar Family Church in Tuscaloosa, Alabama. So every Sunday is our Superbowl. They are big, exhausting, yet somehow energizing days where we get a front row seat to God doing His thing in the hearts and minds of hundreds of people.

Here's the thing about Scott: he's a force of nature. If you could hook him up to the power grid, he could electrify every house in Alabama! But that Sunday morning he was clammy and pale. Like the smoldering coals the morning after a bonfire, the usual heat just wasn't there. But it was a busy morning so I set my worries aside.

That Sunday was extra special because life hadn't been special for a select group of our church family: our 2020 graduates. The pandemic had canceled in-person graduations, celebrations, prom, and pretty much all the fun things we usually do to wrap up the school year. Not only that, but we weren't meeting in person as a church, either. Still, we wanted to bless, honor, and send off our graduates the right way. Some were graduating high school, others college, and still others receiving their doctorates.

We invited a dozen of these exceptionally bright people to interview on stage. The usual warmth, energy, and buzz in our sanctuary was missing, though. Instead, we all sat in front of 600 empty chairs, with only a handful of essential

crew and staff sprinkled throughout the room. But still, we were streaming this graduation service to over 8,000 people online. So even if the crowd wasn't present, we all knew they were with us on the other side of the cameras. Moms, dads, friends, and fellow students enjoying a bit of normal in an abnormal world.

One by one, Scott introduced the graduates as they took their seats on stage and accepted the gift I handed them. The stage was alive with vibrant purple lights reflecting off festive balloons floating behind them. But nothing shone as bright as their smiles. Two of our kids, Destiny and Isaiah, were graduates on that stage, as well. Destiny was graduating from Hillcrest High School and Isaiah his first year at Bethel School of Supernatural Ministry.

Scott shared a short message called "Achieving Through Adversity," commending the students for making it through a tough time. He looked sharp in his charcoal gray suit beneath the dancing purple lights as he worshiped and clapped like the hype man he always is. But instead of his usual effortless enthusiasm, his energy was more like sunshine filtered through gathering storm clouds. I could see that he just looked tired and worn out. Still, Scott encouraged the graduates that they'd made the best of an undesirable situation. He opened his Bible and read Ephesians 3:20 to begin his message:

"Now to Him who is able to [carry out His purpose and] do superabundantly more than all that we dare ask or think [infinitely beyond our greatest prayers, hopes, or dreams], according to His power that is at work within us . . ."

Scott looked up from his Bible and said, "God wants to do things beyond our wildest thoughts and dreams." Then, just beginning to slur his words, he gave the note cards with the interview questions to me, saying, "Pastor Kristi, I'm going to let you ask these questions."

The graduates' easy smiles melted into nervous glances, following Scott as he stumbled toward the back of the stage. Without warning he doubled over, wheezing, heaving, and gagging, starting to pass out. Online, concerned questions started to pepper the comments section on the live feed.

My eyes went wide, chills cascading through my body.

Was my husband sick? Were my kids going to see their daddy pass out from exhaustion? Was this really happening in front of thousands of people?

Every cell in my body screamed at me to turn around and run to Scott's side.

These questions flew through my mind in a flurry, like a tornado whipping through a little town, picking up sheds and roofs and fence posts, scattering debris across once neat and tidy streets.

Every cell in my body screamed at me to turn around and run to Scott's side. I'd never expected this, even though I knew he was exhausted.

I clutched the notecards tightly, trying to keep them from rattling out of my hands. Willing my mind to focus, I asked the questions on the note cards, one after the other, half listening to the students, half listening to Scott wheezing behind the stage. I heard familiar voices whispering around him. It sounded like he was lying down. But was he conscious? Was he speaking? Was he in pain?

Someone put a hand on my shoulder as the students continued to share their answers. It was Pastor David Redding, Daystar's executive pastor. He said, "I'm going to take over for Pastor Kristi."

I spun and hustled to Scott's side.

He was sprawled out on the back of the stage. In the dim light I saw they had unbuttoned his black dress shirt, exposing his chest and upper abdomen. He clutched his chest, and through labored breaths said he felt like someone had slammed a knife into his sternum. Our son, Isaiah, and a couple of other staff members hovered nervously, someone already on the phone with a 911 dispatcher.

Then we noticed the blood starting to pool under his skin.

OH, THE MANY HATS . . .

Leading up to the graduation service, we had been grinding. Hard. We wore so many hats our hat rack didn't have an empty peg left! Maybe you can relate?

Life has a way of overfilling itself. Kind of like when you walk into your garage and notice piles of leaning boxes, unused toys, dusty golf clubs, and that piece of weird patio furniture you're not sure what to do with. Stuff accumulates. Our calendars looked like that overstuffed garage, begging to be organized and reordered. But we were in constant motion, and reflection and pruning were nowhere on the horizon.

We are parents, pastors, and entrepreneurs. Our kids were entering the prime of their lives. Two went to school at Bethel in Redding, California (and as of the time of writing, still do). One of them moved to Fayetteville, North Carolina, one lives in Tampa, Florida, one lives here in Tuscaloosa, and another lives in Tulsa, Oklahoma. From graduations to weddings to grandbabies, we'd found ourselves bouncing from coast to coast.

Our kids are the light of our lives and we're all close. Parenthood hasn't been a walk in the park for the Schatzline clan (more on that later), but we couldn't be more proud of our kids. Nevertheless, loving your kids well and being there for them takes time and energy and many airplane flights. Lots of all of these.

We are also entrepreneurs and were all in on taking our coaching business to the next level. Every week we worked with over fifty clients, helping them thrive in their physical, mental, and spiritual health. Adding to that, we're blessed to have over 100 coaches in our organization across the country. This meant we were training and traveling non-stop. The only real time we had together was on plane flights or road trips. But every person we helped seemed to confirm that we were spending our lives well.

After all, how can you put a price tag on life change? You can't. So we kept a thousand plates spinning at once. When one started to wobble, Scott would get it back on track. And while he did that, I was flying from Zoom to Zoom like a hummingbird.

Oh, and did I mention we also do this other little thing . . . ?

We are pastors. Scott and I have served in many churches over thirty years. From worship pastors in Alabama and North Carolina to staff positions in New York at Times Square Church with David Wilkerson, to lead pastors at Daystar Family Church in beautiful 'Bama! Funny enough, pastoring is a lot like parenting. Only instead of having seven kids, you have over 1,000! It's not a job, it's a calling. It's not a 9-to-5, it's a way of life.

We love our people fiercely—and they love us. But that also makes it hard to stay within healthy boundaries for yourself and make room for rest. This is especially true for Scott. His motto has always been, "It's all about the love!" Loving people and helping them is in his DNA. Y'all, I watched this man serve people at a superhuman level. Sometimes I swore he was going to unbutton one of his flashy flower-patterned dress shirts (that he wears so well) to reveal a giant Superman "S" on his chest.

Scott and I would routinely hold ten or more counseling appointments per day. The unending schedule wore us to the bone. I knew Scott was getting tired, too, but his capacity always *seemed* unlimited, like he could always find more fuel in the tank. I must say we have learned a thing or two about trying to be the "hero" in others' lives. It was purely out of love, but we have realized that only Jesus can fix what's broken.

Many of the people we counseled had a lot of church hurt—meaning they'd been deeply wounded in some way by a church or Christian ministry. Many times, church hurt causes people to view church and its leadership as the bad guys. One bad apple in the bunch can turn people off of church forever. Scott used to say, "You don't quit going out to eat because you had one bad restaurant experience." So our heart was always to help people heal and experience an amazing church community.

It hurt Scott to see people in pain. He is a natural shepherd and wants to help fix everyone's problems. In each appointment he'd listen patiently, crying with people, empathizing with them, and challenging them.

Scott spent nonstop hours taking phone calls, answering emails, responding to social media comments and messages. Even when he wasn't physically with people, he was mentally, spiritually, and emotionally with them. Every new burden became his. That got heavy, but he'd gotten used to it.

What he could never get used to, though, was the pain of racial rejection. Sadly, it is prevalent in our neck of the woods. Scott's dad, Bishop Pat Schatzline, started Daystar decades ago. His ministry always attracted great diversity in culture and ethnicity. Black people, white people, Hispanic people, and everyone in between. We gathered by the hundreds, united in worship, separated by nothing.

For some reason, this ruffled a few feathers.

Years ago, when one of Scott's high school friends met Jesus and started attending the church, some people even quit attending. Why would a new believer cause another Christian to stop attending a church, you ask?

Because he was Black.

Racial reconciliation is part of the heartbeat of our church, which means it's close to Scott's and my heart too. The criticism (even from pastors of other churches) about ministering to a diverse congregation was painful. This is the kind of hurt that digs deep roots because it's a rejection of God's own heart. Did you know the first thing Jesus ever prayed for us was that we all be united (John 17:20-21)?

This drive to unite our church also meant Scott was visiting each of our four campuses every Sunday. He'd preach at one, then dart off to another, and another. We've now become three campuses (English, Spanish, and online) in one location, but this intense Sunday rhythm added to the stress and complexity of our lives.

PASTORING IS A FULL-CONTACT SPORT

Leading a church like Daystar also means having a grasp on the big picture. Vision and fresh ideas poured out of Scott continually. Honestly, our team picked up his long-time nickname: the Energizer Bunny. His brain never stopped. There was always a new way to serve Tuscaloosa and he had increasingly extravagant sermon series ideas.

Now, it might be easy to think, "Oh, new sermon ideas, that's cute …," but Scott doesn't just preach sermons, he engineers productions that stick with people for life. Let me share just one example with you from a few years ago.

Have you ever seen the movie *Nacho Libre* with Jack Black? The main character, Nacho, is a cook at a Mexican monastery that cares for orphans. To raise money to feed them, Nacho becomes a professional wrestler. And in all his "stretchy pants" glory, he tumbles around the ring in a red cape.

Scott loves this movie. One day he had a thought: What if we recreated the set of *Nacho Libre* … in our sanctuary? Yep, that happened.

Imagine walking into church on a Sunday morning and seeing this: Instead of rows of chairs facing the stage, they were organized in four wings facing a genuine boxing ring we rented and set up in the middle of the sanctuary. Rows and rows of church chairs became like stadium seats at an elaborate pay-per-view event! But wait, there's more.

Scott also recruited a dozen actors (and a professional wrestler to train them) to illustrate the message. The main character dressed exactly like Nacho from the movie: blue tights, bright red boots, a lovely speedo, a flowing cape, and of course, a Luchador mask (the colorful masks Mexican wrestlers wear). Nacho then squared off against the enemies we fight every day.

Depression wore a green mask and black tights. Lust wore a yellow cape. Pride sported orange shorts and arm bands.

And a referee in black and white stripes officiated the whole thing.

Between bouts, Scott, the referee, walked to the center of the ring and preached the sermon. He shared about the spiritual strength Christians need to overcome each of these opponents. Finally, at the climax of the sermon, it was time for Nacho to fight the strongest enemy of all, *Fear*. But no matter what moves he pulled or how hard he fought, he was slammed down to the mat again and again.

Everyone in the crowd leaned in as our brave Nacho, representing each one of us in the battle of life, got smacked down. *Fear* would fly off the ropes with an outstretched arm and send Nacho hurtling. He struck the mat with heavy thuds. Sweat poured off his body. And I'm telling you, he was honestly taking a beating in there. Then, just when it seemed like Nacho couldn't get up, Jesus stepped into the ring, helped him up, and took care of business!

I wish you could have heard the thunderous applause. A thousand people went wild all at once, rising to their feet, whistles echoing against the sanctuary walls. It was controlled chaos, with a specific point people have never forgotten: Jesus fights our battles. He's our help, our companion, our friend. And even when life knocks the stuffing out of you, He helps you up, raises His nail-scarred hands, and shows the enemy who's boss.

Just a few years later, on that graduation Sunday, Scott would be the one laid out on the ground, gasping for breath, and desperately needing Jesus to step into the ring with him. All the weight he'd been carrying now pinned him to the ground, suffocating him. Maybe our breakneck pace had finally caught up to him.

WHEN PURPLE DISSOLVES INTO RED AND BLUE

As I knelt beside Scott, joined by several staff and pastors, along with our daughter, Destiny, and two of our sons, Isaiah and Noah, the other graduates were still answering questions. Noah was the first to notice the blood pooling beneath Scott's upper abdomen, creating a massive purple bruise. I heard Danyelle giving our church's address to a 911 dispatcher. The room swirled around me, and Scott grunted between the stabs of pain in his chest and shooting down his left arm and side.

I didn't realize how severe it was until he looked me in the eyes and said, "I'm gonna die, I'm gonna die, I'm gonna die … I love you."

Then his eyes rolled back in his head, exposing the whites. His jaw went slack. Julian, one of our staff pastors who's also like a son to us, shook him by the shoulders and slapped his face, trying to keep him conscious.

"Stay awake, Pop, stay with us!" he shouted.

Scott's color rapidly changed to chalky white, beads of sweat breaking out all across his cold skin. And that's when Isaiah stood up, waved his arms, and shouted, "Turn on the lights! Turn on the lights!"

Pastor David quickly brought the service to a close, praying for Scott's healing and radiating peace, confidence, and calm. Thousands of people had just seen their pastor bent over in pain and heard him collapse. While this left so many questions unanswered, there was one thing everyone knew for sure: we needed God to step in. Big time.

Our lives had been moving at full-tilt—and then, everything stopped.

Three EMTs wearing blue jumpsuits burst into the sanctuary, bringing a stretcher to Scott's side. He was still going in and out, though they found a pulse. They slid him onto the stretcher like they had a thousand times before with a thousand other people. But never my husband. Never my children's daddy. Never Daystar's beloved pastor.

Our lives had been moving at full-tilt—and then, everything stopped. The demands, trips, and campaigns evaporated from my mind. All that mattered was Scott. I ran alongside him as the EMTs wound through the sanctuary and into the parking lot where the ambulance waited.

They slid him in and immediately pulled away. Pastor Julian rushed to his car to take me to the hospital. The ambulance sped out of the parking lot, red and blue lights flashing. It seemed like our life was disintegrating. I had just stood with Scott on our familiar platform beneath purple stage lights. But now, just like the color purple divides into red and blue, we were separated.

Those flashing ambulance lights were a perfect picture of the moment.

Urgent. Telling everyone something bad was happening.

Julian pulled up, I jumped in his car, and we chased after Scott, hurtling toward a hospital I had visited a hundred times before, praying for sick people from our church or celebrating newborns. Things weren't supposed to be this way. But surely God was going to see us through this?

Just twenty minutes before, Scott had prayed these words over the graduates: "You didn't promise to take away our difficulties—but You did say You'll be with us. And that You'll never leave us .... The darkest night, You will light it up."

As we sped toward that hospital with Scott's future unknown, I prayed, "Well, God, we need you to light up this dark night—only please, no more red and blue lights." If only I knew then just how much darker things would get.

Chapter 2

UNDERCOVER NURSE

A strange peace fell over me as Julian followed the ambulance to the hospital. The soft hum of the highway, the towering Alabama oaks whooshing by, the whirring lights of the ambulance. All of it should have terrified me. In hindsight, I had no idea the journey that lay ahead—one we're still walking, even as we write this. But that's what God does. He gives peace where there shouldn't be any. He binds up broken hearts and proclaims favor on His people even in the valley of the shadow of death. He swaps charred ashes for joy, and He does a wardrobe makeover on the mourning, giving them garments of praise (Isaiah 61:1-3).

I don't know what you're going through right now. It may be the darkest, most painful season of your life. Everything might be falling apart around you. Your marriage might be on the rocks. One of your children might be stuck in a lifestyle that's strangling the life out of them. Your closest friends or family may be mistreating you, and you just don't know why. You may be battling cancer or suffering a health crisis. You might have just lost your job, and you're still not sure how you'll make ends meet. You may be struggling with deep depression, just trying to find some hope. Or maybe you feel an emptiness in your heart you can't seem to fill.

Regardless of how great, or how terrible, life may seem right now, I have learned this: everyone is fighting a battle, even if no one else can see it. So what is your battle, my friend?

*Everyone is fighting
a battle, even if no one
else can see it.*

Scott's battle had barely begun. But here's what I know. Following that ambulance should have been terrifying, but it wasn't. Now, it definitely wasn't easy. I'm not trying to sugarcoat or paint this situation in pretty pastel colors. But I experienced peace in that car that I know didn't come from a tough mindset or positive attitude alone.

God met me at the beginning of a trial I never thought we'd endure, and that we still can't fully see the end of. So whatever your fight, here's what I can offer. This promise from Philippians 4:7 is as true for you as it is for our family: "And the peace of God, which transcends all understanding, will guard your hearts and your minds in Christ Jesus."

But I tell you what, the way the next couple of days in the hospital went down, God needed to guard more than my heart and mind. I needed him to guard my mouth, too, because there were *some words* I wanted to say about Scott's care in the hospital that night!

GOING UNDERCOVER

We pulled into the ER entrance just behind the ambulance. Before the car had even stopped, I jumped out, tugged on my mask, and rushed to the EMTs. They had flung the ambulance doors open and were already wheeling Scott through the glass hospital doors that slid open to receive him. Scott was more alert, moving around, and his eyes looked coherent. *We're gonna make it through this,* I thought.

I immediately went into command mode, rushing in alongside Scott and the EMTs, and started to tell the medical staff who met us at the doors what had happened to him. My explanation was abruptly interrupted by a barking voice.

"What are you doing back here?" a security guard said. He held up his hands and stepped in front of me. "You can't come back here with him, we have COVID protocols to follow!"

I stopped, watching Scott disappear into the labyrinth of hospital hallways. I couldn't believe this. My husband had just experienced Lord-only-knows-what in front of our church, my children, and his wife. This is not how it was going down.

"Are you serious?" I said sharply. "That's my husband in there. He's very sick and I need to be with him to find out what's going on!"

I started to walk around him, but he cut me off.

"I'm sorry ma'am, but at this time you need to stay out here."

It was 11 a.m. on a Sunday morning. Usually, we were half-way through morning service. But here I was, fuming and on the verge of saying some very un-pastoral things to a security guard. I clenched my fists and breathed, then turned around. Cars streamed into the parking lot. My children and about forty other people from our church were parking and walking up to me. (Let's just say I was glad I didn't totally lose it right then!)

Love radiated from them like when a warm ray of sunshine shoots through the clouds on a miserably cold day. We prayed, talked, sang, and prayed some more as we waited, like an impromptu church service in the parking lot. An hour passed, then two, three, four, five, six, seven …. We had been there since 11 a.m., and it was now 6 p.m. and I still had no information about Scott. Was he okay? Did he have a heart attack? Was he suffering internal bleeding?

All questions, no answers. Then, as if on cue, a doctor at the hospital, who attended our church, stepped out to our small gathering and walked up to me.

"Kristi, are you alright?" he asked.

"They won't let me in, which is frustrating. I haven't been able to explain anything to the doctors, and they haven't updated me on how he's doing," I replied.

"I have an idea," he said.

He disappeared into the hospital. As he was a doctor, he could come and go freely. A few minutes later he came out with an armload of surgical scrubs.

"Here," he said, handing me the scrubs. "Go put these on, then follow me in."

I slipped them on, pulled on my hat, masked up, and walked behind him like it was my job. I tried to hold a posture that signaled, no big deal, I work here, I do this all the time. It turns out Scott had been admitted into the intensive care unit (ICU). So when we walked in, the nurse at the front desk looked puzzled. But the doctor quickly explained, "Scott is my pastor, so I'm just checking on him."

She nodded and we wound our way back to Scott's room. My heart dropped when I saw him. He was hooked up to monitors and an IV. But worse than that, he looked distraught, scared, and confused. It seemed like he knew as little as I did.

Scott looked up, surprised to see me in surgical scrubs, but he was visibly relieved.

"Honey, are you okay?" I asked, walking to his bedside.

"I'm scared," he said. "I have no idea what in the world just happened to me. But they gave me some very bad news in the emergency room."

My chest tightened and eyes went wide.

"They said I have cancer..."

That word is heavy. As pastors, we have walked alongside dozens of families who have fought cancer and won—and others who lost but graduated to heaven. Grandparents, moms, dads, brothers, sisters, children, and everyone in between. And for the whole day Scott had been isolated, getting fragments of information (or misinformation) from multiple sources. He had been passed around the hospital with everyone's opinions dumped on him without further explanation.

I immediately rejected a cancer diagnosis. We had seen that awful disease too many times to count. I knew that wasn't right.

I squeezed Scott's hand. Then said, "Babe, there's no way this is cancer."

"I told them about how badly my left arm was hurting, the chest pain, my difficulty breathing ..." Scott said. "They knew about all of it and still said the cancer may be terminal."

To say I was angry is an understatement. This treatment bordered on malpractice. Since when is a patient–*who clearly just had a major heart issue*–supposed to care for himself? Scott was trying to recover, cope with pain, describe the situation, and learn as much information as he could. All the while, the threat of terminal cancer loomed over him. This did not create a healing environment.

I worked hard to keep my cool (again), and I tried to be present with Scott in such a whirlwind. He walked through the day, doctors, and potential diagnoses as best as he could remember. We were alone, so I hugged him as tightly as I could and kissed his sweet face, trying to share a moment of peace and connection.

Mid-embrace I heard the door to his room swing open–and a nurse was frozen dead in her tracks. Her eyes were saucers of surprise, shocked to see a nurse kissing and snuggling up with a patient!

"Oh, I'm sorry!" she half-screamed. She practically sprinted away from the room. No doubt going to fill some fellow practitioners in on the juicy romance going down in Scott Schatzline's room. The best part is neither Scott nor I ever said anything about the incident because we didn't want me to get kicked out. To this day she probably thinks some mystery nurse had the hots for a patient. But it was me, Scott's undercover nurse, ready to get some straight answers from this yarn-ball of a situation.

I only got to be Scott's undercover nurse for about five minutes before I had to leave. I kissed him one last time and followed our doctor friend outside. Some of our dearest friends, Wayne and Courtney Pendel, had just pulled in. As soon as they heard about Scott, they dropped everything and drove four hours from Fairhope, Alabama to Tuscaloosa.

The rest of the night was a blur. But Wayne and Courtney, Pastor David and Cindy, Pastor Shannon, and our kids didn't

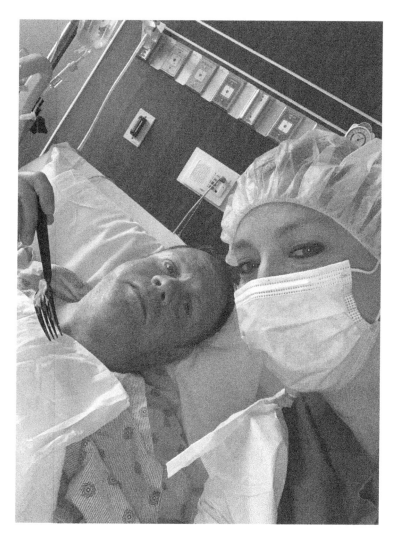

leave my side. They helped me settle into a hotel just across the street—and even set up a mini coffee bar in my room. To say they were a blessing is the understatement of the century. They kept me functioning. Courtney helped me assist the clients in our business. And she was the first shoulder I cried on.

I'll never forget laying in my hotel bed next to her. It was like the weight of what had just happened dropped out of the sky onto my chest. My hands began to shake and I sobbed. And she was there, a safe harbor in troubled seas. This would become my pattern. I'd be strong, positive, and vigilant around Scott. He would never see me cry, or doubt, or scream, or drop my face into my palms in frustration. But I had a handful of people who knew us, loved us, and could support me by simply creating space for me to be real. In a sense, they have been part of my healing even as Scott healed. And oh, how I needed it, especially that first Sunday night with Scott in the ICU.

WE ALL NEED AN ADVOCATE

Hospital rooms are now my (Scott's) least favorite place on Earth. I don't remember much after collapsing at church that Sunday morning, but Kristi says I was scared. Very scared. She said I tried to explain to the doctors and nurses the fiery pain in my left arm. I described how my chest felt like a knife was stabbing me over and over again when I collapsed on that stage. But nothing I said made any difference. The cardiologist told me I had the heart of a thirty-year-old. Nothing was wrong with it. They said it was a mesenteric artery rupture, which is an artery deep in your abdomen.

Apparently, that could get fixed with surgery. Okay, great. Let's do this thing and get it fixed, right? But the surgeon said I likely had terminal cancer. So if they operated, the cancer could spread throughout my body. I would go from bad to worse. I felt like a broken toy no one could fix. Alone and afraid. Hooked up to IVs and monitors, stuck in a sterile room. And I couldn't even see anyone's faces, just their eyes. Concerned pair after pair of eyes. Everyone looked the same, even though they all said different things.

My mind kept racing. If I had cancer, was this going to be it? Wait, what did that nurse just say again? When was the next doctor coming? Why are we sure my heart is okay? Because of COVID, Kristi couldn't be with me. I had to work through all of this by myself. I'd never missed her so much. I needed my sweetheart with me. But she was stuck at home (as they weren't allowed in the waiting room) getting second-hand information from nurses' phone calls (if I was lucky).

It was upsetting then, and it's upsetting now. Talking with Kristi, I realize just how awful it was for her, too. If I imagine our roles reversed, and she was on her own after collapsing in front of our kids, staff, and church, I would go crazy. But looking back, there's one thing I know for sure: my wife is freaking Superwoman!

She snuck into the hospital to be with me. She paced for hours in the parking lot, waiting for updates that never came. She tried to keep conflicting information straight. And she kept our business, family, and church family together at the same time. She's an amazing person. But we know our experience wasn't the only one like this during the pandemic. This was the story for everyone.

There were people who died alone. Funerals delayed. And very likely people who passed away because they had no one to advocate for them. It absolutely breaks my heart to know so many people were–and still are–in pain. They're dealing with deep depression. They feel isolated, like no one is there to stick up for them. And I know there are many people who had it worse than we did.

Kristi advocated for me as best she could. She reminds me of what John wrote about Jesus in 1 John 2:1. He is our advocate, which means someone who comes alongside you to help. We all need an advocate, especially when we're in a hospital bed.

From my experience I can tell you, never feel bad about pushing for all of the information you can when your loved one is sick. Whether they're a husband, wife, parent, child, or anyone else, no one is going to get them the care they need better than you. I'm thankful I had my Kristi Love, even if she was on the outside of the door.

The most connection I got with her, and my kids, was my daughter, Destiny's, virtual high school graduation on May 19, 2020. I had been in the hospital for two days and was missing a huge life event. It killed me to not be there! I had to watch on

FaceTime as she and her friends made the best of their filmed, ceremony playback (that really wasn't much of a ceremony at all). They had great attitudes and had as much fun as they could. Her daddy was supposed to be there. She is a sweetheart and tried to make a memory for me to have with them, to be included, at least a little. But all I could do was watch her on a blurry video. It broke my heart. And I didn't know it then, but that was how life was going to be for a long, long time. My family was living their lives with a missing father.

ALONE IN A WHEELCHAIR

Scott was finally discharged after five days. I (Kristi) will never forget picking him up in the same entrance where the EMTs had rushed him into the hospital. There was a low awning where cars can pull through, and there in the shadow was Scott, slumped in a wheelchair, sitting on a dirty curb. No nurses. No attendants. Nobody at all. There was no debrief or next steps. No one to help him get from the wheelchair to our vehicle. I could see he was utterly exhausted. This whole week had taken a tremendous toll on him.

We were supposed to have a series of follow-up appointments. But they were either confined to clunky telemedicine visits because they didn't want anyone on site, or they were canceled. I'll admit, that peace God had given me, that warm spiritual comfort, was threatened by anger. The entire situation felt unjust.

However, we have walked with God since we were children. We've encountered the miraculous. We have prayed for sick people and they've been instantly healed. We have seen broken lives restored. We know our God and believe that

> **Our faith has constantly been tested. But as many times as it's challenged, God proves to be faithful.**

He does things we could never imagine, even in situations we never expected to be in.

Our faith has constantly been tested. But as many times as it's challenged, God proves to be faithful. He is a safe place to take fear, anger, and any other ugly emotion. He is big enough to handle what you're going through. He doesn't always pluck you from the fire. But He does walk through it with you.

Scott and I both knew this even from the day we met. Just a couple of kids who loved Jesus—and fell crazy in love with each other. Scott's week in the hospital had been bitter, but the vast majority of our life together had been sweet. For that, I am grateful.

Chapter 3

TABLE FOR TWO

*G*rowing up, my (Scott) family didn't have two nickels to rub together. But that never kept my mom and dad from serving everyone they could. They were pastors who loved all people, which is why our house was constantly filled with people we didn't know! As kids, we never knew their exact story. Some were homeless and needed a warm bed. Others were hungry and needed a meal to fill their bellies. And still others needed an escape route out of a bad situation.

My mom brought people home like kids find stray puppies! If they needed someone to love on them, the Schatzlines' door was always open. This kind of love can't help but rub off on you–and all of us kids, my older brother Pat, older sister Reneé, and I, all caught the love bug. Although, we all expressed it in different ways.

Even though my parents were feeding three growing kids and themselves on a tight budget, they fed the people who stayed with us, as well. So there were always many mouths to feed. So our family volunteered at the food pantry. I remember night after night going to the pantry after school and loading up families, single moms, and anyone else who couldn't feed them-selves with boxes of food. Then, once everyone was through for the evening, our family got to take home the leftovers. This continued from grade school all the way into junior high school.

We ate a lot of canned goods and boxed food. But our favor-ite was always when there were a few bags of M&Ms, candy bars, or potato chips left. We'd split them three ways, eat some,

and tuck a few bags away. Pat and I both took them to school, but we had differing philosophies for what to do with them once we got there!

Everyone knew our parents were pastors. And I had developed a reputation for talking constantly about Jesus, loving people, and living an upright life. I wasn't a religious kid by any means, blaming and shaming. I just genuinely loved people and it hurt me to see kids suffering or not walking in God's love. So, I found a way to do something about it, coaxing kids into some better behaviors.

Our school, Gardendale Junior High, was just like any other, and the athletes had the worst potty mouths! To this day I just don't cuss. It's not that I think anyone who does is bad, but it was never part of my vocabulary. So I would wince whenever I heard basketball, football, baseball, or any other players cursing blue streaks that would make a sailor blush. That's where my stash of candy came in handy.

I'd tell the athletes, "Listen, if you stop cussing, I'll give you M&Ms and candy bars. But if I hear you talking like that, no candy for you!"

Turns out, even junior high athletes are eager to watch their mouths if candy is involved. So week after week I handed out bags of candy to the kids who stopped cursing. And they were always quick to out anyone who was secretly cussing. It was actually a lot of fun and made everyone feel just a little bit better about themselves.

Now, let me tell you about my big brother's candy habit. He's always been the entrepreneur of the family. Honestly, he's a big reason why Kristi and I started the businesses we run together today. He has this knack for sniffing out opportunities. So, being the businessman he is, Pat brought his bags of candy and set up shop, selling them to kids and making nice pocket change in the process!

The kids, of course, caught on. So whenever they saw Pat opening up shop they'd ask, "Where's your crazy brother? He gives the candy away." Pat would shrug and kids would have to pony up the cash. I like to think that Pat met needs in different ways! But no matter what happened at school, all three of us kids were heavily involved in the life of our church.

THE STRANGE MAN IN WHITE

Pat had a funny way of describing me. He'd always say, "Scott could get the Devil saved!" I wouldn't go quite that far, but our family was serious about spreading God's love everywhere we went. My parents always showed us that it wasn't what we did on Sunday mornings that mattered, but how we lived during the week. The Church (which is the people) always needed to leave the building. Although this looked a little different for my family.

You see, we actually *lived* in an old church building! Pat's room was in the baptismal and Reneé and I had makeshift bedrooms off of the sanctuary. It worked well enough; however, not only was our family there, joined by frequent guests we were helping out, but hundreds of church mice lived with us, as well. I remember one month we actually caught sixty mice. They would scamper all over and you could hear them in the walls at night. And whenever it rained, all of our rooms would flood, so we kept everything off the floor that we didn't want to get waterlogged.

This church-building-turned-house was near the new church building where my family ministered. It was in the middle of a field, no trees, just lush grass that stretched as far as we could see. As kids you never think about it, but I'm sure this living situation was inconvenient for my parents. On the plus side, all we had to do was pay for the utilities and minor upkeep. However, some months even that $300 stretched us thin. Because, of course, my parents would even give their meager salary away to people they thought needed it more.

One month, after they had blessed a family with every penny we had, there was more month left than money. But the bills were coming due. The lights and water wouldn't pay for themselves, and it was down to the wire. On the last night of the month our parents were invited out to dinner (we thought maybe that family wanted to help us out, but it turned out they asked my parents for money instead). So that evening it was just Reneé, Pat, and me at our little church house.

The sunset bathed everything in a golden light. Our house was set far back from the highway, so anytime a car would drive up you'd hear and see it before visitors ever made it to our doorstep. This evening a strange thing happened. We heard three sharp knocks on the door.

We were sitting in the living room, then all sat up and looked at each other.

"Did someone just knock on the door?" I asked.

"I think so," Reneé said.

"They must have walked up here," Pat guessed. Honestly, it was a little creepy. So Pat and I did the brave thing and made Reneé go answer the door!

The old floorboards creaked under her feet as she walked to the front double doors. She opened the door cautiously and saw a man wearing flowing clothes. He was handsome, kind, and peaceful, putting Reneé at ease. Through a smile he asked, "Is the master of the house home?"

Reneé started to laugh. Obviously, that was a bizarre question.

"You mean my dad?" she asked.

He pulled out a sealed envelope from his robe. Then said, "Would you make sure he gets this?"

She took the envelope, looked at it, then looked back at the man in surprise. "Okay," she said. She shut the front doors, still wondering what on Earth was going on. Then quickly realized she hadn't thanked the man–southern manners and hospitality run deep! She opened the front door again and said, "Thank you …" but trailed off.

The man was nowhere to be seen. There was no dust kicked up on our dirt road. No taillights moving toward the highway. It was dark, quiet, and we were the only people there. It was impossible for him to have disappeared in the split second she had closed and opened the door. She stepped onto the stairs and scanned the field once more, then came back into the living room.

Pat and I had heard a man's voice but couldn't make out what he had been saying. But before we could even ask what it was all about, we noticed the surprised expression on her face and the mystery envelope in her hands.

"You'll never guess what just happened," Reneé said. She filled us in on his strange white robes, odd questions about the master of the house, and sudden disappearance. Then she called our parents and told them the same story.

"Well, open the envelope," my dad told Reneé. She slid her thumb across, breaking the seal. It crinkled as she pulled it open. Inside, we saw three crisp $100 bills. Pat, Reneé, and I looked at each other in disbelief.

"Dad, there's $300 in here!" Reneé said.

It was exactly the amount we needed at just the moment we needed it. An eleventh-hour gift that we couldn't explain. I'll never forget that moment. It was such a reassuring feeling that no matter what happened or how desperate the situation, God knew what we needed. He understood down to the dollar what it would take to keep the lights on. He saw every secret act of generosity.

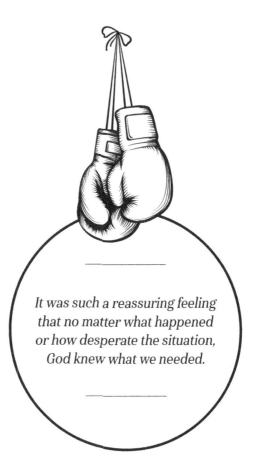

It was such a reassuring feeling
that no matter what happened
or how desperate the situation,
God knew what we needed.

He knew every church mouse scampering through the old church building. He understood the constant sacrifices my parents made. And most importantly, He knew that we would all need to hold on to that miraculous provision moment.

If you're reading this, you know that life gets hard. Really, really hard. Nights get dark and when we need help most, it seems like it's too far away. But even when we can't see anyone coming, I know firsthand that God is in the field with you. There is an angel waiting in white on the blackest of nights. This doesn't make it easy. The waiting between need and provision can be incredibly painful. It stretches faith and challenges your endurance. You think, *this is too much pain ... too much sorrow ... too much fear.*

Kristi and I have had those same thoughts. But we've been visited by a God who's never early and never late. His timing is frustrating at times—but it's perfect. As of writing this, when we reflect on the last eighteen months of our lives, we've been through a pandemic, my Sunday-morning collapse, kids moving across the country, grandbabies born, and a whole bunch of awful stuff we're going to share in the pages ahead. But still, we remember so many situations where God has shown up. We trust that He'll keep showing up.

We've also seen that God doesn't care who you are or what you look like. He simply wants your heart. A lot of times, especially in the South, we get caught up in appearances. Or we feel disqualified because of things we've done in the past. Have you ever felt like that? Like certainly God wouldn't want anything to do with someone like me. I've done way too many bad things, I've said hurtful things, I haven't helped when I know I should have.

Well, let us fill you in on a little secret. The same God who's willing to send an envelope full of $300 to a little church building in the middle of nowhere wants to show up to your rescue, too. No matter where you're at, what you've done, or what you look like. God only has one *type* he's looking for—someone who looks up and says, "Help."

WHO WILL SIT AT THE TABLE?

Imagine this scene at our church, Daystar, one Sunday morning. The sun streams into the foyer through high windows as the building fills with lovely people. The coffee is on, and conversation is buzzing. People are hugging, high fiving, and getting ready to find seats in the sanctuary. Some of the men have suit jackets and some of the ladies wear happy sundresses. Others are dressed casually in t-shirts and shorts. There are Black people, white people, Asian people, and even Spanish-speaking people because that's one of our campuses that meets at the same time in the adjacent building. You can find just about every kind of person imaginable here.

Then, out of the corner of your eye you catch a bedraggled man shuffling in. People notice him one by one, watching him amble around out of the corner of their eyes. He pours himself some coffee and scoops up some food, even looks around in the trash cans. You don't want to stare, but you can't help but see there's a trail of dirt that's followed him in. He's got matted hair, an unkempt beard, and a grungy hoody, wearing a backpack stuffed to the gills. He stands out like a sore thumb. But still, it's church. Come as you are, everyone is welcome, right?

The band starts playing and the crowd moves toward the sanctuary. Everyone flows into the hundreds of rows of seats, and as you walk to an open chair, the grungy gentleman walks by, and you catch the overpowering smell of a dumpster. The lights dim and you take your seat as the worship music swells, and the guy moves on somewhere else. Pretty soon, you forget all about him.

The band walks off and people carrying tables, chairs, candles, and centerpieces walk onto the stage. A few more follow them and suddenly the stage has transformed into a five-star restaurant. I'll never forget watching everyone's eyebrows raise as I walked out, dressed like a maître d', and began to welcome guests into the restaurant.

The first patron is a woman named Michelle who hands me an invitation while desperately trying to hold back tears. She follows me to her table, then a waitress comes to take her order. While they speak softly, I read Michelle's story out loud to everyone in the congregation (who is looking *very* confused, by the way!).

"Meet Michelle. She joins us this morning in a lot of pain. She cried her eyes out all night, feeling deep guilt and shame. Last evening, Michelle had an abortion. And today, she isn't sure that was the right decision. She can't talk to her family, because she's scared they'll reject her. She can't talk to her friends or coworkers, because she's worried they won't understand. She definitely can't go to church, because she's worried they'll judge her. What can she do now?"

As I read her story, a man wearing a suit and tie came into the restaurant and sat down at a nearby table. Another waiter came out to him, took his invitation, and set a glass of wine down on his table before taking his order. I introduced him.

"Meet Jeff. He's recently divorced and now only gets to see his kids every other weekend. His wife left him when she discovered that he relapsed and his dependency on alcohol was consuming everything. He's now in a downward spiral. He looks okay on the outside, but inside he's a wreck. His hands shake if he goes too long without a drink. And all he can think about is getting enough alcohol to bury the pain. He knows it's only a matter of time before his boss finds out or he's pulled over while driving intoxicated. Jeff has tried to quit a thousand times, but his life's a mess. Is he too far gone?"

Another woman was seated while I read Jeff's story. She had a hood tight around her face, but she pulled it down when she was seated. Everyone in the congregation gasped. She had deep purple bruises under both of her eyes and another deep cut across her cheek. Blood trickled from her nose. Another waitress took her invitation and then her dinner order. By now, Michelle, the first guest, had gotten her food. Her silverware clinked as she ate. And Jeff's food arrived as well.

"This is Stacy," I read. "She is living in her car right now, running from an abusive relationship. Her boyfriend started getting physical with her, but she doesn't have any family or friends nearby to help her. He threatened to hurt her even worse if she tried to run, so she stayed. The pain and the fear were finally too much, so she mustered up remarkable courage and ran for her life. However, her boyfriend controlled all of the money. She didn't even have a chance to pack clothes or toiletries. Stacy is alone on the streets, scared sick that her boyfriend will find her and things will get even worse. Where can she go now?"

One by one, seven more people were seated at tables. They each had an invitation and a story. A teenager secretly dependent on pornography. A young, professional-looking woman dependent on painkillers. Everyone who joined me on stage was in agonizing pain. Some feared for their lives; others feared they had permanently ruined their lives. But everyone was united in their hurt, loneliness, and despair.

Then, as I finished reading the final person's story, the scruffy looking man who had wandered in at the beginning of service walked onto the stage. But a waiter walked over to him, put his hand up, and asked him to leave. You could hear their conversation.

"Sir, I'm going to have to ask you to leave," the waiter said. "We have a dress code and you're simply not presentable. If you'd like to order, we can bring you some food in the parking lot. But you can't eat inside looking like that."

The man walked away and I turned to the congregation.

"Every one of these people is hurting," I said, gesturing toward the ten people eating on stage. "But could you ever tell? They look put together. Their clothes are clean, their hair is tidy, they know how to hide what's going on inside. You see, my friends, everyone is fighting a battle you can't see. The problem is when we judge based on what's happening on the outside when we can't see their hearts. We don't see them weeping late into the night. We have no idea they are hiding their hurt."

The sanctuary was dead quiet; I let the silence hang. You could hear footsteps walking from the back of the stage. It was the homeless-looking man again. The waiter met him, "Sir, I'm sorry, but we can't allow you in looking like this—"

The waiter stopped talking as the man threw back his hood and unzipped his sweatshirt. He let it fall to the floor, revealing a white robe with a blue sash. The man's hair fell around his shoulders as he walked past the stunned waiter and sat down with Michelle, the woman who had had an abortion. She broke down in deep sobs as the man held her hand and talked quietly with her.

The man was Jesus, and let me tell you, there was not a dry eye in the place. I said, "We have a habit of looking at the outward appearance, but God looks at the heart. Did you know that in Jesus's day He was rejected and unwelcome by the religious folks? They said he hung out with the wrong crowd. He didn't do the right things and he said the wrong things. But I wonder, do you think if Jesus was walking around physically today, we would invite him in? Do you think he would look how we expect him to?"

"Did you know that he was homeless? He said in Luke 9:58 that foxes have dens and birds have nests, but he didn't have anywhere to lay his head. Here's the message this morning: no matter who you are, what you've done, or what you're going through, God has a table for two set for you! Jesus is giving you an invitation to meet Him, to be loved and accepted by Him. You're never too far, because he's in the business of rescuing broken people. Just like me, and just like you."

That morning people jumped out of their seats and filled the altar (the area at the front of the sanctuary surrounding the stage). They wept and prayed for each other. There was a profound sense of healing that morning. God met us right where we were. We all felt His pure love and it broke some serious chains off a lot of us that day. We don't shame people into God's family. His kindness draws us in.

A PLACE FOR YOU

I saw my parents live this way every day. If there was a need, they would meet it. If you needed a bed, we had a little old church building and a warm bed with your name on it. (As long as you don't mind being roommates with a mouse or two.) They taught me to love people, to hurt when they hurt, and remember that everyone is going through something hard.

There's a place for you at God's table. Jesus is waiting for you to join Him. Kristi and I have shared this hope with thousands of people over the last few decades. We've had the great honor of welcoming people into God's family who thought they were too far gone. Or others who believed lies about themselves, thinking God wouldn't have anything to do with them. We've stepped into a lot of people's hurt. But I have to tell you, something changes when *you* are the one who needs a seat at the table.

As 2020 wore on, we had no idea how much harder things were about to get. We had to hold on to every miracle like the stranger in white showing up at our church-building house. Every time He healed our family from sickness, or the deep hurt we experienced when my sister Reneé passed away. Collapsing on the stage on that graduation Sunday, May 17, 2020, was difficult. But we hadn't even set foot in the valley.

All we could do is remember that empty seat at the table with our name on it.

There's a place for you at God's table. Jesus is waiting for you to join Him.

Chapter 4

THE GOOD FATHER

I'll never forget the day my (Kristi's) daddy, Olen Kizziah, bought me a fiddle. It felt so perfect in my small hands. Its smooth curves and light spruce body tucked gently beneath my chin, my little arm extending down the neck, little fingers pressing on the strings. The way the bow made the whole instrument sing was magical. It vibrated with excitement and sang–just like me! I'm sure my first bow strokes sounded like a dying rabbit, shrieking in the forest. But songs came quick and my joy at playing came even quicker.

I grew up singin' and fiddlin' in our family band, BJ Holloway and the Sour Mash, alongside my daddy who loved pickin' and grinnin'! We played bluegrass and country gospel, traveling from town to town, hall to hall, church to church, playing anywhere and everywhere we could. For me, the stage always meant pure joy. I felt more at home standing there in front of big crowds and a handful of people alike. And the more gigs we played, the more instruments we collected.

I got a drum set alongside my fiddle and microphone. Then a guitar, mandolin, keyboard, and on it went, all along the musical alphabet. We played fast and loud, smiles never fading. One of my favorite venues was the Palmetto Barn. It was exactly what it sounded like, a barn with dirt floors, rough wooden benches, and the worst acoustics you can imagine, smack dab in the middle of nowhere. What it lacked in fanciness it made up for in sheer energy. It was a cramped space that rang hollow as the night's bands tuned up and decided on last-minute set orders.

But the sound grew warmer as people piled in, and the driving fiddle and mandolin solos blended with the hoots, hollers, and stomps of a bunch of people thoroughly enjoying themselves.

This was my life every Friday night, from ages eight to fifteen. But BJ Holloway and the Sour Mash wasn't only a Friday night affair. Gigs filled weeknights, as well. We played venues like the pre-Civil War Tannehill Opry in McCalla, Alabama. Folding chairs scraped across its concrete floors and our notes bounced from metal wall to metal wall. But they had my picture there, their favorite fiddle-playing girl. The audience made me feel like a star there. We also sang at a nursing home every week with a rotating cast of whoever was available, playing mostly country gospel tunes and old hymns. It brightened the elderly folks' long, slow days and curbed the edge of loneliness we knew many felt.

While the stage felt like home, performing was my second-favorite part of our musical family life. My first, and most cherished, was seeing the way my daddy looked at my mama, Judy, when she sang. It was like the world stopped. His eyes nearly twinkled as her sweet voice soared over his nimble fingerpicking patterns. On stage, our family seemed perfect. A beautiful mother, handsome father, and cute-as-a-button little girl smiling, laughing, and in harmony. But these brief, happy moments weren't ever quite enough to make up for the bad ones.

MY HIDING PLACE

The mixture of my daddy's guitar and mama's voice was my favorite sound in the world. But do you want to know what the worst sound was to me? It was the sound of old truck tires crawling up the gravel driveway at night. The hollow thud of the driver's side door slamming, and the scraping footfalls of my daddy's boots as he stumbled, drunk, into the house. It was the worst sound in the world because I knew what was coming. A radically different man than the one I performed music with was entering the house.

I learned to watch for the signs. If his truck wasn't in the driveway when I got home from school, I knew we were in for a miserable night. This meant he had stopped to have a few beers. So I walked in our backdoor with a pit in my stomach and let my backpack slip off my shoulders, at least easing one weight before we had to endure the shouting, the hitting, the fighting. On these days, there were no gospel medleys at home; our soundtrack was sorrow. But

> **Growing up in an abusive household teaches you to become a shadow.**

this was so conflicting, because, like many alcoholics, my daddy was a wonderful man—when he wasn't drunk. He imparted words of wisdom—when he wasn't drunk. He was a godly man—when he wasn't drunk. When he wasn't drunk, he would plant a dusty boot on the open tailgate of his truck, leaning his forearm against faded jeans, and pour out his heart in gentle bursts. I'd experience my real father: tender hearted, compassionate, and loving. But this man would disappear whenever a bottle touched his lips.

Growing up in an abusive household teaches you to become a shadow. You listen for telltale hints of raised voices or tense conversations. And as anxiety fills your body, you run to any secret safe place you can. Because you know the screaming, beating, and violence is about to explode.

I'll never forget the moments when my mom said just the wrong thing to my dad, setting him off. His rage would flare like a forest fire, hot, intense, and destructive. She collapsed to the floor, covering her face and crying, but the only thing that stopped him was my older brother hitting him on the head with a literal two-by-four. And this is when I ran to my secret place, tucked away under the kitchen cabinets.

I've always been small, but as a mousy little girl I could fit in the tiniest spaces behind the pots and pans. I'll never forget the old cabinets' musty smell mixed with dish soap residue. And the closed cupboard doors muffled the sounds of violence as I hugged my knees tight against my chest, burying my face into my legs, crying and scared and alone. I also knew to expect the confused feeling of being hugged and apologized to by the man who'd just hurt my mother and brothers and sister. He never hit me, but I got his words.

The happiest times were when we played music, because he never drank. He never hit, screamed, or disrespected my mother. He just looked at her with love and awe as they made music together. I so desperately wanted that musical man to be my full-time daddy. So much so I would beg him to just hug mama and tell her that he loved her. If he just offered the smallest thread of affection, I thought, things could finally be okay. But he waved me off and kept searching for peace in a bottle—peace he never found. While kids are resilient, abuse is trauma so deep and knotted it's nearly impossible to untangle.

As a child, all I could do was make it through our trauma moment by moment. You can't predict when it will end. And honestly, it feels like it never will. You're stuck in a cycle of kid-like joy while playing and having fun to the hair-trigger explosions of anger and terror. Seeing my mama hurt like that made me feel helpless, and even guilty, for not being able to help her. Even as a young girl, though, I watched the life slowly fade from my mother's eyes. Like a long-setting sun, getting dimmer until it was all but snuffed out. As I reflect on these moments, I realize they are where my strength to punch back was forged.

OUT OF THE WOODS

"Mama," I called, one evening after she and Daddy had had a massive fight.

"Mama, where are you? I need to show you something!"

My little feet pattered from room to room, clutching some trinket or picture I'd drawn that I wanted to give to my mom. The kitchen … empty. The living room … empty. Her bedroom … empty. I ran to a window, stood on my tippy-toes, and looked out through smudged glass. Maybe she was in the garage? Empty.

My mom wasn't in the house because, lost in a deep depression, she had walked into the woods and tried to take her own life. Her hurt was so severe that life was unbearable. Her pain was bigger than her hope for living. It crushed me—and to this day, still crushes me to think about. A woman, wife, and mother pushed past the point of a desire to live, even for her own children. As I write this today, so many decades later, my own children's faces flash through my mind. And I realize how dark that place would be to desire death over life. There is no judgment for this; it simply hurts my heart.

Eventually, they would divorce, but somehow, like magnets, no matter how broken they were, they kept coming back together, getting remarried after the abuse, trauma, and harsh words that could never be unspoken.

My siblings and I watched the family drama unfold. And while I can't speak for them (as they had to bear the worst of it), the only safe place I found besides music was church. We had to grow up gritty, like sandpaper that never wore out. But deep down, I always knew this strength wasn't just me. There was a greater power seeing me through these seasons. At seven years old, I went to the old-fashioned altar at Yellow Creek Baptist Church and gave my life to God.

A GOOD FATHER?

This led to one of the most powerful moments of my life just three years later: I was filled with the Holy Spirit in the very church where we pastor Daystar today! However, that was simply the first step in a long journey of trust. Because while I came to know God as my Father, Jesus as my Elder Brother, and the Holy Spirit as my Comforter, I couldn't seem to unhitch my view of God from my experience with my dad. My earthly father looked mad most of the time. So all I could see in a father was an angry man sitting across the kitchen table, wagging his finger disapprovingly, listing all the things I wasn't, slinging my failures and faults at me like mud that stuck, then hardened into clay.

When I read my Bible, or prayed, or raised my hands in worship, an image of an angry dad in the sky lurked like dark storm clouds sweeping in from far away. Always threatening to break out in a furious thunderstorm. While it took years, God healed this broken image by showing me, day by day, year by year, his kindness, mercy, and compassion.

Jesus told a story in Luke 15 about two brothers and their very different relationships with their father. The younger brother wanted his inheritance early so he could go party it all away. But back then, in the first century, it wasn't like the family inheritance was sitting in a 401(k) or bank account. Inheritance was tied up in property, livestock, or the family business. This meant the father had to sell half of everything they had to give this money to his youngest son. Worst of all, inheritance was only passed down when the father died. So, in effect, the younger son was saying to the father, "I'd rather have your stuff than have a relationship with you."

The older brother, though, was the goodie two-shoes. He stayed home and behaved. He did his chores, said his prayers, went to church, and never cussed! (He was probably *almost* as good of a kid as Scott was!) So the oldest boy stayed and the youngest left home to party away half of everything his family had worked for—and that's exactly what he did.

Then one day, when all the money was gone and his "friends" ditched him, he found himself working in a pig pen. He was so destitute that the pig slop looked appetizing. Shame overcame him. The mud between his toes seemed like a direct reflection of who he was: dirty, unclean, and unlovable.

Have you ever felt that way? Like the things you've done—or maybe some things that have been done *to you*—have made you unlovable? Like maybe forgiveness is for everyone else but you? Like God's mercy is a gift you'll never find beneath your Christmas tree?

I have. I did. A few years after giving my life to God I was touched inappropriately by someone outside of our family we had trusted. I didn't understand it at the time, but this crossed a boundary I didn't know how to repair. So I allowed boys in middle and high school to push further physically than I was comfortable with. This left me feeling so guilty and ashamed.

> **I hid my sin and shame and guilt, tucked it far away.**

Really, I felt like that younger son in the pig pen, realizing that he'd gone too far and there was no way home.

I hid my sin and shame and guilt, tucked it far away. I was scared to be open and honest about these issues. No one needed to know the real me because they would catch on. They would see I was dirty and full of sin. My siblings always thought I was the goody two-shoes because I was the baby, but deep down, I *knew* better.

So there I was again, in a cycle of seeing God as an angry Father who saw everything I did, heard every word I spoke, and saw how damaged I was. There was that pig-pen mud, squishing between my toes. But Jesus's story about the two brothers didn't stop there.

You see, the younger brother realized that his father was at least a fair man. And that maybe, just maybe, he could return home and become a servant in his house. At least he'd have a clean bed, water, and food fit for humans to eat. So in his ragged, dirty, smelly clothes he returned home. No doubt he was rehearsing his apology with every step.

I'll bet many of my prayers for forgiveness echoed his ...

Father, if you'll just forgive me, I'll never do that again ... Jesus, if only I could feel your love, I'll live perfectly for you ... Holy Spirit, if only you would fill me up like you did when I was ten, I could be a faithful servant ...

But something surprising happened to that younger brother as he returned home.

Before he could speak a single word of apology, his father ran to him on the road, not even waiting until he walked up the front porch, and he wrapped him in one of those bear hugs only a happy daddy can give his child. And he wouldn't hear a word of making his son a servant–instead, he threw a feast, saying, "My son that was dead is now alive!"

You see, it took many years, but when I finally saw that God is *like that*–meeting us in our dirt and guilt and shame, tucking His strong hand beneath our chin and lifting up our eyes to meet His, and welcoming us home as full sons and daughters–my relationship with Him radically changed. While my earthly father was broken and flawed, my heavenly Father was whole and loving. My heavenly Father would never raise His voice to shame me, Never wag a heavenly finger in disappointment, Never raise a menacing hand at my mama or siblings.

Even more surprising, I had always thought the older brother in Jesus's story was the good guy. He stayed home and kept in line. He brought honor to the family and didn't let boundaries get crossed, right? Well, it turns out, it's not so simple. You see, instead of celebrating that his little brother was alive and had returned home, he complained to his father about the celebration. He said, "Father, I stayed home, I did everything right—but where is my feast? Where is my inheritance? Why don't I get what I deserve?"

And right there we see something icky. The older brother only wanted his father's stuff, too. He just went about getting it in a different way. He tried to behave his way into an inheritance. It turns out, his heart wasn't any more pure or noble than his younger brother's, he just knew how to play the game.[1]

So if you've ever lived in shame, feeling like that younger brother who'll never measure up, or never be able to perform your way back into God's family, I get you. I understand. But I also pray you take Jesus's parable about those two sons and that wonderful father to heart. We have a dad who's ready to meet us on the road, wrap us in a bear hug, and welcome us home.

NOT PERFECT, STILL GOOD

God is a good Father, but his children can still be a little (or a lot) rascally. Church set me on a path to thrive in life. But it wasn't without its issues. I watched people in the church go through messy divorces and secret affairs (that didn't stay so secret!). In fact, even one of the young girls I would catch rides with to church or youth group was taken advantage of by our pastor. I've seen the destruction the enemy can bring into churches and families. It's devastating. But still, God is faithful, and He makes a way for healing, even in all the mess.

Incredibly, the church building that Scott and I pastor Daystar in today is the same church I went to from nine years old through high school, where so much of that junk happened. So when I tell you that God can bring restoration and reconciliation to any place, I mean it! Honestly, I shouldn't have made it through my childhood and adolescent years without major dysfunction.

---

[1] For more insight into the parable of the prodigal son, check out Timothy Keller's wonderful book, *The Prodigal God: Recovering the Heart of the Christian Faith.*

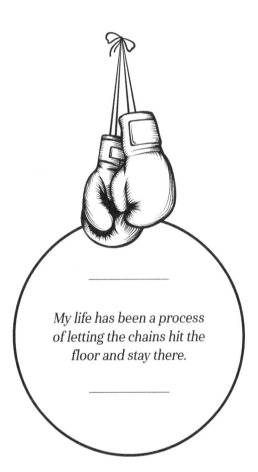

My life has been a process of letting the chains hit the floor and stay there.

I would frequently think, "God, how can you use me after every-thing I've been through?"

However, God has always gently reminded me that we all spend time in grave clothes, but it's our choice whether or not we keep them on. My life has been a process of letting the chains hit the floor and stay there. My past haunted me for a long time, and almost kept me from the best thing that ever happened to me. Because not only did I struggle with the things that happened to me and my siblings, and the tragic things I saw happen in our church, but I came face-to-face with people who liked to dig up my past. They put labels and restrictions on me. But I thank God that one year at summer camp I met a boy in a pink shirt that God would use to change my life forever. All I had to do was catch him!

Chapter 5

FIGHTING FOR LOVE

*S*ummer camp was my (Kristi's) absolute favorite time of the year!

Every year, I could hardly wait for it. And when it did arrive, it just didn't last long enough. I can still remember the long van ride filled with church friends singing funny songs, laughing with excitement and expectation. This week was going to be filled with endless games, pool time, team competition, and new friends blended together to make some of the best memories of my childhood. I may not have attended church faithfully, but I wasn't going to miss summer camp. And there was no place like Camp Ambassador in Clanton, Alabama.

The camp was at the end of a dusty gravel road, nestled beside a pine forest and lily-covered pond. The old chapel showed its fair share of use, the front patio was worn smooth from thousands of kids' feet scampering up and down. But the real excitement happened when, after arriving, you found out your cabin assignment. The girls had a ring of twelve cinder block cabins on one side of the camp, and the boys had one on the other side. You know Christian summer camps, you gotta keep the boys and girls apart—we even sat separately during chapel services!

Can you see it now? Ten bunk beds crammed into each cabin, suitcases, backpacks, sleeping bags and pillows everywhere, all while arguing over who would get the top bunk. This was an annual rhythm of life for me from age ten through my teen years. And for Scott, even longer, as his dad, Brother Pat, was the camp coordinator. They went for more than one week because they served on the camp staff every year.

While I have many happy memories from those weeks, I'll never forget what happened on the first day of camp when I was ten years old. We had just arrived, gotten checked in, and it was lunch time. All the kids lined up along the cafeteria walls waiting for our turn to pick up our lunch tray.

Then, there he was, standing opposite of me across the cafeteria. The cutest boy at the camp, wearing his pink polo button-down shirt, tucked neatly in his khaki pants, matching belt and shoes, and accessorized with one of those pink sock ties. (Do you remember those?).

His blonde hair, neatly parted down the middle, tumbled down near his shoulders, curling out with wings. Everyone wanted to sit next to him at lunch. He was pretty popular. You could just see it. I asked some of my older friends that had been to camp before, "Who is that?"

She looked at me and said, "That's Scott Schatzline."

I know it sounds crazy, but at ten years old, I said to myself, "I'm going to marry Scott Schatzline one day." He was twelve years old, and I was in love!

> **I know it sounds crazy, but at ten years old, I said to myself, "I'm going to marry Scott Schatzline one day."**

It was obvious he was different, at least not like any of the boys I had met before. He was confident, but so sweet. He cared about everyone around him. He had no idea who I was, and probably didn't even look my way when I passed him with my Little-Orphan-Annie curls, face scarred from chicken pox, crooked teeth, and goofy laugh that could be heard across the room. It was an *awkward* season of life!

Every year, outside of the powerful chapel services and altar times, there was a big event at the end of each week: the camp banquet. The banquet was the height of the little camp romances that blossomed quickly (and faded even quicker when everyone went home, as we didn't have cell phones to stay in touch).

Scott had already chosen his date to the banquet. He asked Shelly to go with him. She came to camp with our group. I was pretty disappointed that I didn't get a chance to go with him.

No problem, I thought. *I'll just follow him around the camp all week.*

I wasn't being creepy, but I may have taken a film full of pictures of Scott playing baseball on my cheap, disposable camera. Then, after a long day of games and competition, it was almost time for chapel. We had some free time before camp choir practice (I was always in the choir). I was trying to meet up with Shelly before chapel.

She and Scott were hanging out with some friends around the back of the building when Shelly yelled, "Kristi, get your ass over here!"

I was startled and Scott's eyes went wide as saucers.

"What did you just say?" he asked.

Shelly, acting cool, said, "Yeah, I told her to get her ass over here."

I couldn't help but smile and feel giddy inside. *Wrong move, Shel!*

Scott was strait-laced and so serious about living right with God he was basically John the Baptist without the camel's hair jacket—though honestly, that boy could've still pulled it off. So he was sensitive to words or behaviors that veered off the straight and narrow. And unfortunately for Shelly, Scott was not a fan of cussing.

"Well, I won't go to the banquet with a girl who cusses," Scott said, without skipping a beat.

Scott just walked away, and Shelly was dumbfounded.

The camp bell rang, signifying it was time to go to service. And it was time for the biggest part of the team competition, the talent show. Some guys played guitar and some girls sang. They were all pretty good, but Scott was great!

He took the stage and sat behind a table. Something covered his arms and another boy crouched behind him. After he sat, Scott plopped his arms down on the table. He had stuck them through a pair of pants, so it looked like he was short with spindly legs that wouldn't stop wiggling.

The room instantly started to crack up. Then came the real fun. Two scrawny arms (belonging to the other boy) popped around Scott's body and set out shaving cream and a rubber razor. Scott was giving us a display of how to shave. The arms wildly sprayed shaving cream all over Scott's face with exaggerated, flamboyant gestures. Then scraped it off with the other hand, leaving Scott with a face full of shaving cream and left the whole crowd in stitches! He's always been quite the entertainer.

Everyone loved it, and inevitably, Scott was voted camp king (for probably the third year in a row). After the banquet, we experienced a powerful move of God in chapel service. Then, as quickly as it came, it was over. The next morning, we all loaded up in our vans and buses to head to our homes spread across the South. Scott went his way, and I went mine.

I spent the next five years going to summer camp looking for Scott. I would find his dad, who we called Brother Pat. I would ask him, "Is Scott here this week?"

He would say, "No, he's coming next week."

Then finally it happened, it was the summer of 1988. A lot happened that year. I was fifteen and looking more … let's say … womanly! I made sure to re-introduce myself to Scott. He had a pretty serious girlfriend, but I didn't let that stand in my way.

I walked into the chapel, sat down on the pew in front of him and his girlfriend and said, in my sweetest Southern Bell tone, "Hey Scott! We met five years ago at camp. That was the year you did the shaving cream talent show act."

"Oh yeah, that was a great year," he replied, smiling. "How are you enjoying camp so far?"

Even at sixteen, Scott had a pastoral effect. Kind, loving, sweet, and selfless.[2] He was so easy to talk to and be with (though I know his girlfriend wasn't happy with our instant connection!). I knew I was in love with Scott Schatzline but didn't know how it was going to pan out.

That summer, God really showed me how much he loved me. Not only did I know Scott's dad, Brother Pat, but I got to meet his mom, Sister Deb, and his brother, Pat, Jr. Later that year I met his sister, Reneé, when she toured the state and came to our city, singing with the All-State Youth Choir. I've always felt like God set this entire mission up just for me. I had no idea just a few months later what God had in mind.

THE KENTUCK FESTIVAL

Every fall the sleepy little town of Northport, Alabama wakes up and hosts thousands of people excited to hear music from hundreds of artists, take in fine art, and enjoy homemade food of every kind. It's the Kentuck Festival, and to date it has been going for over fifty years. Hundreds of white tents filled with smiling artists showcasing their handmade pottery, beautiful paintings, chainsaw sculptures, elaborate quilts, turquoise jewelry, and every variety of crafts imaginable, line the meadows between yawning pine trees.

The October after my summer camp of love and reconnecting with Scott, my family band, BJ Holloway and the Sour Mash, was performing at the festival. There were multiple stages and hundreds of bands. As you wandered through the festival tents, tables, and exhibits, you'd weave in and out of pockets of different music. Near one stage you'd hear bluegrass tunes, and further along, country bands with lilting lap steel guitars.

---

[2] I mean, no exaggeration, years later when we were married, Scott literally saved two children from a burning house in North Carolina–this is the kind of guy he's always been!

Late that afternoon, we took the stage. A large crowd gathered as the last rays of sunlight filtered through the pine boughs. Little kids danced in the front with parents and grandparents. Everyone was smiling, clapping, tapping their boots in the dirt, and singing along as we performed the final song in our set, "Girls Night Out" by the Judds. But midway through the second verse a couple from my church caught my eye.

Recently, this husband and wife had all but damned country music to hell. For whatever reason, they thought the Devil's favorite playlist was one country song after the next. The thing about teenage Kristi (and probably still the same today) is that I had trouble suppressing a rebellious streak–especially when I felt people trying to manipulate and control me. So, instead of feeling self-conscious or uncomfortable for singing the "Devil's favorite songs," I belted even louder, singing straight to my undoubtedly offended fellow church members.

The moment we finished I marched straight off the stage and made a beeline toward them. In my most sugary sweet, innocent Christian-girl voice I said, "Hey! How are y'all doing? Did you enjoy our show?"

They smiled a nice, stiff, religious smile. "Oh yes, it was very nice," the wife said.

I could tell she was forcing politeness, but the conversation took a surprising turn. You see, it had been a while since I'd been to a church service, probably hadn't been since summer camp. I'm afraid my summer camp fire for the Lord burned down into smoldering coals a few weeks after getting home. My spiritual life was on-again, off-again. Even though I was only fifteen, I carried a pastoral gift. I just didn't know it yet.

So I asked, "How's the church?"

"Did you hear that we got a new pastor?"

That was news to me. "No, I hadn't heard. What's his name?"

The husband looked up and off to the side, scratching his head. "Let's see, it's an odd name. Something like Pat Shatz-pine? Or Shotz-line?"

My jaw just about hit the dirt and my heart started to pound hard and fast.

"Pat Schatzline? As in Scott Schatzline's daddy?" I asked.

"That's it!" the husband said. "Really wonderful family."

But I wasn't listening anymore. My first thought was, I gotta get my life right with God if I want Scott to have anything to do with me! My vocabulary was more Shelly-like than saint-like, so I knew I had to clean up my act.

As the couple turned to leave, I asked, "When are they coming?"

The wife replied, "Their first Sunday is tomorrow!"

Needless to say, I showed up to church and haven't missed a Sunday since.

TEN DAYS LEGAL

Throughout high school, I never lost my interest in Scott. I was dating a guy at the time Scott's family came to pastor our church. I had to drag my boyfriend to church with me and at this point we were plunged into some form of teenage drama. We had just finished service on a Wednesday night, and I was an emotional basket case. Scott had prayed for a young man at the altar, and I steered my boyfriend over to him, asking if he could talk with us about our relationship.

To this day, I have no idea what he said to us. I couldn't do anything but cry. But I wasn't crying over the relationship of my current boyfriend, I was crying because I was thinking, "Why can't I be dating Scott instead of this poor guy?"

After Scott's mini-counseling and prayer session we headed into youth service. The little corner classroom had theater-style seating. And the youth pastor was welcoming all of us and everyone was finding their place to sit and getting their Bibles out. We were hungry for God's word to be shared with us. Something was changing inside of me–and something outside was about to change, as well. Because about five minutes into class, my boyfriend went to the restroom and never came back. He ditched me at church without saying a word.

Usually, I'd be irate at a boy treating me like this. However, that night, I just smiled my little country-girl smile and floated over to Scott with sad puppy eyes. I had a brilliant idea! I explained my situation and asked him if he could take me home, as my boyfriend was my ride. He immediately obliged (even though he had to find a friend to drive us to take me home).

And so it began.

Scott and I started dating just before he graduated high school. We were just a couple of kids falling in love. However, after graduating high school in 1989, Scott received an opportunity to work with David Wilkerson in New York at Times Square Church, one of that era's most impactful ministries. He served as an intern and played his trumpet in the orchestra and worship ministry.

He had many personal mentor moments with David Wilkerson as they would talk and walk the streets of New York, he served and preached in the homeless shelters, ministered to the drug addicts and the prostitutes on the streets. Love was his language, just like Jesus.

So we dated from a distance for a couple years while Scott served in New York. He lived in one of the theater dressing rooms and only had a pay phone in the back hallway to call me.

I don't know how many thousands of quarters he dropped into that phone, but it was enough to keep us talking every day. And he gave up meals just so he could pay his long-distance phone bill. We actually wrote long letters to each other (mine filled with hearts and smiley faces, no doubt). And even though we were thousands of miles from each other, we both grew deeper in love with each other *and* God's call on our lives.

Fast forward to September of 1990. Scott was still serving in New York. One of the times we got to see each other was whenever he came home for a holiday, or in this case his brother's wedding. We traveled to Lakeland, Florida at the rehearsal. Scott pulled a fast one on me and proposed! He asked me to be his wife, and I immediately said yes, almost hyper-ventilating with joy and excitement. Scott didn't feel he was supposed to stay in New York. Even for all the amazing things God was doing through his ministry, Scott couldn't shake the feeling he was supposed to come home for good.

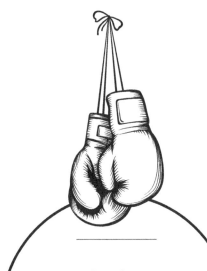

Even though we were thousands of miles from each other, we both grew deeper in love with each other and God's call on our lives.

So, just ten days after I turned eighteen, and two months before I graduated high school, I became Mrs. Kristi Schatzline! Looking back, we were practically babies. We couldn't decide on who we wanted to be in our wedding party, so we ended up with ten bridesmaids and ten groomsmen. The best part, though, was that we skipped my senior prom to honeymoon at Disney World. However, my joy was also mixed with fear. Because not everyone in our lives was on board with this marriage.

I remember judgmental looks from older women. And I can still hear their whispers–spoken just loud enough for me to overhear.

"That girl is damaged goods …"

"She's not good enough for Scott …"

"She'll never really be a Schatzline …"

"I feel sad for Scott, getting tied down with her …"

"This marriage won't last a year …"

My insecurities bubbled to the surface. Like that little mousy girl so many years ago, I wanted to run and hide beneath the cabinets. So I would take a deep breath and remind myself that the little girl had grown up and gotten herself married to the man of her dreams. I wasn't about to let the Enemy or anyone else steal my joy. Over thirty years later, he still hasn't. It also helped that we were happier than any two people on the planet.

We were stuffed in a tiny trailer home filled with borrowed furniture and whatever food a high school girl could muster up. Scott was working at Daystar as the minister of music, and

I was a receptionist at a doctor's office. I would go to school until noon and then work the rest of the day. Scott's running joke was that if I didn't get my homework done, he would make me ride the bus to school! But I managed to pull it off. After graduating high school we graduated to a bigger apartment, and eventually our first home.

We bought a fifty-year-old 1,000 square foot Cracker Jack box of a house. And like Scott's childhood church-building home, it was crawling with mice. We could hear them skittering in the walls at night. Mice or no mice, it was soon time to start filling the house with children. And that's just what we did.

FIGHTING PLANS TO STEAL, KILL, AND DESTROY

We had our first two sons, Ethan and Noah, while living there. Ethan came along in the middle of a very musical season. We were recording the first Daystar worship album. Scott led worship and I sang. So our weeks were filled with a constant whirr of rehearsals, recording sessions, and then mixing tracks late into the night.

 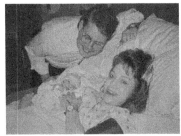

One evening, right in the middle of recording, my back started to ache. Not a normal kind of pain, as if I slept wrong. This was different, and it came with a stomach ache and fatigue. Scott still had a long night of album mixing ahead, but I was just too worn out. So a friend offered to drive me home but made a stop at Wendy's to grab the guys some burgers. In the drive-through line, my pain started to get so intense

I could barely speak. It eased up and we dropped off the food to the guys.

My friend took me home and we decided to call the doctor.

"Kristi, how are you feeling?" He doctor asked.

"I'm–" I winced with pain and started to cry. "I'm–" I tried again, before bursting into more tears.

"Young lady, you need to get to the hospital right now. You're in labor!"

These were pre-cell phone days. So my friend rushed me to the hospital at about midnight, and then went to the church building to get Scott there before Ethan was born. He made it just in time. Within the hour, Ethan Zachariah Schatzline was born. It all happened so fast there wasn't even time for pain medication.

He was born a healthy, content baby. Bringing him home was one of the most wonderful, yet terrifying, things we'd ever done. I think we checked on him about every ten minutes the first few nights. We tiptoed into his room, held our hands just above his face, waiting to feel his warm breath on our fingers. However, one night, our snuggly, calm Ethan began to wail at exactly 2:00 a.m. He wasn't simply crying; these were blood-curdling shrieks. This screaming cry happened for two weeks straight at 2:00 a.m. every night.

Scott and I knew there was more to this than a crying baby. I scooped up Ethan and instantly began praying the name of Jesus over him. I invited the Holy Spirit's power and peace into the room and worshiped in warfare. This happened night after night. Ethan would cry out to me, and I would cry out to God. Until finally, one night, I took Ethan to our living room and sat in our rocking chair. Singing, praying, cooing, holding him tight against my chest.

That's when I saw them. Angels. Broad shouldered, powerful, standing so tall they disappeared into the ceiling. They moved in military formation as if on patrol, walking through our living room where I sat with Ethan, then into his nursery. I walked toward his room and watched as the lead angel plucked up this monkey figure and threw it straight through the window, out of Ethan's room, like it was nothing. The Enemy wanted to infest our house with a spirit of fear, but the Lord went to battle for us. Ethan never faced terrors in the night like that again. And two years later, as a toddler, he became a big brother to our second son, Noah Elijah Schatzline.

Noah faced significant challenges from the moment he was born. After delivering him, the doctor immediately knew something was wrong. Instead of drawing his first breaths and crying, he was silent. Instead of turning a healthy pink, he was turning blue. Both of his lungs had collapsed. They rushed to get him on a breathing machine. However, we didn't know if he would gain the strength to breathe on his own or if the oxygen deprivation had caused any damage to his brain.

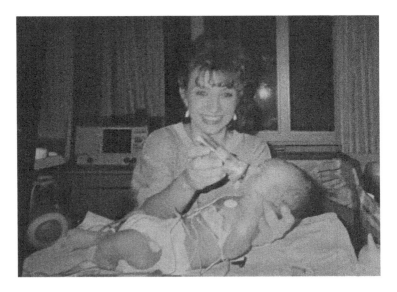

I (Scott) found myself in the hospital lobby with a single Ficus tree standing near a window. There were probably thirty to forty church members and family there praying with us. I laid beneath the tree worshiping and praying through tears: "God we just need one word from you. Will our son live?" I released him to the Lord at that moment and said, "God your will be done."

As the words left my lips I looked up at the slim Ficus branches full of beautiful green leaves, but one single, stark-white leaf was fluttering down like a Holy Spirit dove. And I heard the voice as the leaf fell toward my face: "Just as death cannot attach itself to this tree, neither can death attach itself to your son."

His promise came true. Noah lived. Out of all of our kids, Noah has fought death the most for his entire life. He's had more near misses, car accidents, and battles with severe anxiety, depression and even suicide attempts. And I know why.

The Enemy has tried to steal him because he has a powerful call on his life, as each of our children do. But that, my friends, is the Devil's playbook: kill everything with life, steal anything that belongs to God, and destroy the plans He has on our lives. In Kristi and my early years together, the enemy tried to steal our marriage and joy with whispers of doubt and disqualification. He tried to destroy our security in the Lord by sending dark forces to Ethan, at his most vulnerable. And he threw everything he could at Noah to take his life.

> **I laid beneath the tree worshiping and praying through tears: "God we just need one word from you. Will our son live?"**

Kristi and I are here to say, when the enemy attacks you, your family, or God's plans for your future and hope: *Punch Back*! Lace up the boxing gloves of the promise in James 4:7: "Submit yourselves, then, to God. Resist the Devil, and he will flee from you."

I have meditated on this verse many times since my major cardiac incident on that graduation Sunday, May 17, 2020. It nearly left me dead. But like always, we kept punching and partnering with heaven. However, little did we know that the Enemy was setting up the ring for the biggest fight in our family yet.

Chapter 6

HAPPY FATHER'S DAY

*I*t was Father's Day, June 21, 2020, and we were making up for a spring of missed celebration. Outside, laughter echoed over the glass-calm water of our favorite lake as they paddle boarded, boated, and swam beneath the hot summer sun. Dozens of freshly graduated high school kids, parents, and friends joined us at a beautiful cabin to celebrate the weirdest graduation year any of us had ever experienced. 2020 brought plenty of surprises, and a virtual, socially distanced graduation ceremony was one of the many disappointments among them.

Add to that, we had delayed Destiny's graduation party because of my (Scott) May 17 incident (on graduation Sunday, no less). And I'm so heartbroken to say it was further pushed back because my beautiful mother–with a royal name fit for a princess–Ila Deborah Jean Adkins Farmer Schatzline, passed away in early June.

It was soul crushing. This had truly been a string of life-changing events you expect no more than once or twice a decade in just one month. My father, brother, and I were devastated. And honestly, it was especially hard for me because I am, and always will be, a mama's boy–and proud of it! (Jesus was a mama's boy, too, y'all). She was full of grace and wisdom and had lived her life fully sold out for Jesus. She also gave me my crazy sense of style, always buying me new clothes and making my dad mad.

For real, though, there wasn't a person in Tuscaloosa who didn't know who she was. She and my dad's ministry through Daystar helped so many thousands of people over the years. The pain was intense, and I cried myself to sleep many nights. I was also worried about my dad. Unless my dad was off planting churches in China (where there were often warrants out for his arrest and officials opposed to Christianity chasing him through the streets), he and my mom were inseparable. He lost a wife, a ministry partner, and his best friend.

Because Destiny's graduation party was just a few weeks after her passing, our celebration was mixed with moments of grieving. And of course, for a little extra drama, I had emergency gallbladder surgery four days earlier!

So we had been a pressure cooker of trauma, sorrow, and now joy. At least Destiny and our other Daystar high schoolers were enjoying some normalcy together. Plus, we figured we had already walked through the fire and come out the other side. Today was going to be a good day for our family and me, as long as I could sneak in a little rest and recovery time. My kids even blessed me with a new golf club I had been eyeballing for months for when I hit the links again soon.

However, if there's anything I've learned, it's that for every one mile of road, there are two miles of ditches. As it turned

out, we'd just begun walking our mile and there was still plenty
of ditch left.

"WHAT ELSE COULD GO WRONG?"

With how things had been going, I (Kristi) didn't think this
graduation was ever going to happen. But the lake house we
ended up hosting the party at was a miracle in more than one
way. The owner, Dr. Brent Tidwell, is an elder at our church,
close family friend, and very successful chiropractor in our
area. He owns a beautiful home right next to this one that he
and his wife AirBnB. But it's such a popular place it was booked
through the entire year when I asked about it a month prior—
except for the exact two days we wanted to host the party!

We took this blessing and set up party HQ the day before,
allowing Scott plenty of time to rest as we were joined by other
close friends and Daystar pastors, David and Cindy Redding. In
fact, that morning, we were eating breakfast together, smiling,
laughing, and talking about what a crazy first half of the year

it had been. And Scott laughed, shrugged, and said, "Hey, what else could go wrong?!"

We were about to find out.

That Father's Day afternoon, we didn't know it at the time, but Dr. Brent's son-in-law had a medical emergency at their house next door. It appeared that he had a heart attack, so he had to administer CPR for the first time (outside of regular training) in fifteen years. They rushed his son-in-law to the hospital, and with the COVID-19 situation, thought it would be hours before he could even be seen by a doctor. Miraculously, he was in and out of the emergency room in under two hours—and back resting at their house that evening.

During this same time, Scott began having severe shoulder pain. But he grunted through it, entertaining our friends and guests, telling stories and sharing the many things God was up to through our lives and ministry. I was flitting around like a butterfly, refilling the punch bowl, laughing with friends, and keeping an eye on Scott.

I had an odd feeling, because he looked clammy and pale, a lot like he did when he collapsed at the graduation Sunday service a month before. It was almost like there was tingling in the air, like something was about to happen—and suddenly it did.

As the evening drew near, most of our guests had left except a few close friends. Scott was acting like he felt good; he had showered and was ready to sit down in the living room and have a cup of coffee. Then, suddenly, everything changed.

DEATH RATTLE

All I heard was a *thump* followed by Cindy's voice screaming in the living room: "Pastor Kristi! Pastor Kristi!"

I flew around the kitchen counter and wove through the stunned guests, darting into the living room. Scott was crumpled on the floor next to the fireplace. I rushed to his side, and he tried to speak, partially coherent.

"What, baby?! What?" I said, shaking his shoulders. "Scott, talk to me. Talk to me!"

In reply I heard the most horrifying sound of my life—I can still hear it, even as I write this. A vibrating, almost electronic gurgle sounded from his mouth. His face was slack, he was white as a sheet, and cold to the touch. His body seized and the sound, called the death rattle, wailed. Humans make this sound when approaching death, which I later learned happens within twenty-four hours.

For the second time in a month, my husband was dying in my arms. But this time was different. He was totally unconscious and might as well have been a million miles away.

"Call 911!" I yelled.

I turned and saw Pastor David sprinting out of the front door, making a beeline for Dr. Brent's house. But instead of mass panic, the room erupted in prayer. Destiny burst into the room and immediately locked onto Scott and spoke life over her daddy: "Scott Schatzline, you will live and not die in the name of Jesus! Breathe life right now!"

> For the second time in a month, my husband was dying in my arms.

She repeated this with the confidence of a queen with an army at her back. Declaring over and over that he would live, despite seeing her father's lifeless body in front of her. Within ninety seconds, Dr. Brent, who had returned from the hospital with his recovering son-in-law just half an hour ago, scrambled to Scott's side, immediately giving CPR for the second time that day.

You could hear Scott's chest pop beneath the compressions, ribs flexing out of joint and his sternum cracking. But that's what it takes to keep a heart beating. I began to shake and had to leave the room, knowing there was nothing I could do for him except work with the medical team who was *hopefully* just a few minutes away. However, a few minutes turned into twenty before the Carroll's Creek fire department was able to arrive.

We were quite a ways out of town and at the end of winding forest roads along the lakeside. When the team arrived, Dr. Brent had been performing CPR for over twenty minutes straight. He was like a machine, never pausing, tiring, or missing a compression. A paramedic knelt right next to him and Scott, and said, "I'm going to trade with you in three ... two ... one ..."

The paramedic seamlessly took over the compressions as he and the other two talked precisely about what would happen next. He ripped Scott's shirt off, placed pads on his chest, and yelled: "Clear!"

Scott convulsed as he shocked him. I was in shock, too, staring at my dying husband while surrounded by presents, balloons, and streamers. His skin began to gray, contrasting with the bright Hawaiian leis we wore to celebrate. The paramedics got a faint pulse–but Scott wouldn't open his eyes again that evening. They placed him on a gurney and rushed him into the back of an ambulance.

FOURTH PERSON IN THE FIRE

The siren whirred. The red and blue lights flashed. And again, I got into a car with Pastor Cindy as she followed the ambulance carrying my husband to the hospital.

Tears streamed silently down my face. Cindy has an incredible way of peace about her. She spoke life, prayed, and kept positive. But there was no naiveté about what was happening–there was a very good chance my husband would die with my final words to him being about punch and party favors.

Why didn't I take him in? Why did this happen again? Why are you letting this happen, God?

Questions raced through my mind and the tears kept coming. But the last thing I remember praying, as we pulled in front of the ER was, "God, even if Scott does not survive this,

I trust you. Even if you don't answer our prayers, I know you're in control. But I'm begging, just like with Shadrach, Meshach, and Abednego, stand as the fourth person in the fire, Jesus."

THE FAMILY ROOM

For the second time in a month, I watched my husband disappear through the automatic doors of the emergency room. And for the second time I wasn't allowed in with him. COVID restrictions locked everything down, which meant I had to wait on the curb, wondering if my husband would live or die. Was he still breathing? Had he woken up in the ambulance? Would he be in a coma?

Some of our close friends waited with my kids and me. Praying, crying, shocked. I was disappointed every time someone in scrubs walked by without any report. Until, a couple of hours later, a nurse locked eyes with me. I couldn't see her expression behind her mask, but her body language spoke volumes: something is wrong and I'm here to tell you.

"Kristi, the doctor would like to see you in the family room after he knows more. Why don't you come in and wait there?"

My heart sank. Tears ran down my face. "I *know* what the family room is for." My voice quivered. "I'm *not* going into that room! Just tell me right now, is my husband going to live?"

The family room is where you're told about how hard your mom, dad, brother, sister, husband, wife, or child fought—but sadly wasn't going to make it. This room had the residue of sorrow and hollowness. The family room wasn't about reuniting, it was the place where the grief process begins. I've stood in this room with other families many times. Praying with them. Holding them. Loving them. And I had a front row seat to their tragedy.

I just couldn't bear the thought of life without Scott. My husband, my kids' daddy, and a powerful man of God ... about to be gone? This couldn't be happening.

"I'm sorry, ma'am," the nurse said gently, "but that's the best I can do for you right now."

Evidently, I followed, because my next memory is sitting in the bleak family room with faded paintings of fields and flowers and bridges on the walls. Outdated issues of *National Geographic* and *People* magazines sprawled across the tables. But all we could do was sit, wait, and pray.

It was nearly 10 p.m., and every minute that ticked by seemed like hours. We waited all night. We shivered, questioned, and cried until there were no more tears. Silence settled on us until the doctor finally came. He looked exhausted, as well. We stood and leaned forward, ready for any news at all—good or bad.

"Scott is in critical condition," he said. "He's in a coma and we have to take it one day at a time."

I had no idea the towering mountains we would climb over the next twelve months (and beyond). No one did. The doctors could not tell me what to expect. People don't survive this type of cardiac arrest. But he was alive and that's all that mattered. Finally, the next morning after a procedure in the cath lab, the doctor let me see him briefly as he was en route to the ICU.

The doctor explained that, for the moment, Scott was sedated and on a ventilator. Already, a few doctors had begun working on his case, but they needed to consult specialists in Birmingham. Scott had suffered a worst-case heart attack, called a widow-maker, as well as a sudden cardiac arrest. We would learn that less than one percent of people survive this mother of all heart attacks, and it was only because he had lost eighty pounds and radically transformed his physical health in the five years leading up to this moment. However, as the doctors continued to guess at what might lay ahead, two things came through: *they were in over their heads and some of them didn't even seem to care.*

They spoke about Scott like a Sunday crossword puzzle. His case would sure be nice to solve, but if not, that's just how it goes. They could wait until the next puzzle rolled through their doors and try again. For now, it was time to ship him off somewhere else and let him be their problem.

I am angry at them for this. Not just for myself, but for the countless families who have to walk through such deep trauma, confusion, and pain.

Obviously, not all doctors are like this. We have since been blessed to work with some of the best, most caring doctors in the world. But the callousness was a bitter pill, hard for me to spit out. As Scott has worked so hard to recover (as you'll see in the chapters ahead), I've also had to work on my heart. Releasing anger, especially when it is justified, does not come easy. However, even that day I vowed to the Lord, "We will take what the enemy has meant for death, destruction, and despair, and walk with God to turn it into songs of joy, peace that surpasses understanding, and hope for greater things."

> **Releasing anger, especially when it is justified, does not come easy.**

As Scott always said, "It's time to move from now into your next."

Whether he was awake or sleeping, that is what I intended to do by my husband's side. It would be a fight for every inch of progress, but I wasn't about to let death win over a man with so much life left to give.

THE RESURRECTION STONE

Have you ever wondered what people remember when they're in between life and death? I (Scott) can tell you because I died on the floor of that lake house. My heart stopped pumping and oxygen was cut off to my brain. We don't know exactly how long, but it was long enough for me to experience something so real and profound it nearly defies explanation.

First, I will tell you that Dr. Brent Tidwell saved my life. I thank him and tell him I love him every chance I get. But in between the moments he was running to my side from his house to where I collapsed, I went to another place: Heaven.

There were lots of different colors, twinkling like perfectly cut gemstones reflecting pure light. God was there. I couldn't see his face, but I could see the most brilliant blue light surrounding him, too bright to look at. The best way I can describe it is by sharing what Moses saw in Exodus 24:10: "Moses and Aaron, Nadab and Abihu, and the seventy elders of Israel went up and saw the God of Israel. Under his feet was something like a pavement made of lapis lazuli, as bright blue as the sky."

It was like floating in a gorgeous blue ocean of peace that met with the brightest blue sky you've ever seen. As beautiful as this was, I remembered something of what had just happened to me.

"God, I am so mad at you," I whispered. "I've loved you my whole life. I've done everything to honor you and share Jesus with hurting people. How could you let this happen to me?"

A deep voice rumbled: "Scott, do you want to go back?" I told God, "Yes, I do." God said to me, "I love you and I'm bringing you back to use you as a living testimony greater than ever before."

This promise didn't immediately cure my anger or hurt, but to this day nothing can erase this profound experience from my memory. God met my anger with his peace and made a promise to me. And I know my God, He never fails and always keeps promises, even if it looks different than we planned for.

Sometimes it's okay to ask God why, sometimes He gives you the answer, but most times He allows you to operate in the faith that comes from Him to begin with.

There is also something special in that lapis lazuli-like stone that Moses, and now I, saw with God. You see, to me, the stone contains a resurrection promise in itself. Lapis lazuli is mostly made of a gorgeous, blue mineral called *lazurite*. I believe there is a subtle message there. Jesus once had a dear friend named Lazarus who passed away–but he wasn't about to let him die.

God met my anger with
his peace and made
a promise to me.

His sisters sent a message to Jesus, "Lord, the one you love is sick" (John 11:3).

Jesus responded, "This sickness will not end in death. No, it is for God's glory so that God's Son may be glorified through it" (John 11:4). But then, his friend Lazarus died. How could this be? Why would he let a man he loved—and who loved him—die? Especially after *promising* it wouldn't end in death, but glory?

Jesus didn't let this resurrection moment escape. He went to his friend's tomb and had the stone, signifying death, rolled away. Then, "Jesus called in a loud voice, 'Lazarus, come out!' The dead man came out, his hands and feet wrapped with strips of linen, and a cloth around his face. Jesus said to them, 'Take off the grave clothes and let him go'" (John 11:43-44).

I will tell you; this event is much easier for us to read than it was for Lazarus and his family to live. Kristi and I don't share our story with you lightly. We're not here to pat you on the back and say, "Don't worry. Don't cry. Everything will be fine. Just trust God and smile."

We're actually here to talk to those still in grave clothes … the ones going through death or trauma … and say, this is not easy. No matter how much life people speak over you, or how many Bible verses get texted to you, it is very difficult to be the person whose life has just changed forever.

You may question God, like I did, wondering, "God, hello? Where are you? Did you leave us?" It's easy to stay angry and bitter, and to even lash out at the people around you just trying to help. That is why I am so grateful for a woman as wonderful and powerful as my Kristi Love. She walked with me and helped me remember that just like her, God had never left.

It can be so hard to take off the grave clothes when it seems like all you've seen is the backside of a gravestone, rolled in between you and your old life. But as we have learned, sometimes what was has to die for God to bring you into your next.

I don't say this lightly. And if you're going through this, I don't even expect you to believe me right now. But please stay with us and cling on to hope. Because when I finally woke up, hope was very hard to see. However, it was all we had.

I died and met God–but He sent me back for greater things. As you'll see, though, our lives would never be the same.

Chapter 7

THEN HE SMILED

"*I* *will shoot straight with you,*" *the doctor said to me (Kristi),* *his voice muffled through a facemask.* "Scott will never be the same. I don't believe he will ever walk or talk again—and he may not even know who you or your children are. Frankly, I'm shocked he's still alive. He should have died."

These are not the words a wife wants to hear about her husband. But this is what one of the physicians told me as Scott laid in an ICU bed in a coma in the early hours of the next morning. We learned that Scott's widow-maker came from one of his arteries being eighty percent blocked—and another being one hundred percent blocked. His heart was working hard, but the blood wasn't flowing like it should have. And Scott was still in desperate trouble.

I felt hollow. It was a sleepless night filled with tears, anxiety, and desperate pleas to God. And honestly, I couldn't believe this was happening. How on Earth could so many awful things happen so fast?

Barely two months before, he'd collapsed in front of our children and our church. A few weeks after that, his mother passed away, sending tides of sorrow and depression over our hearts. Shortly after, Scott had his gallbladder removed in an emergency surgery. And just four days later, on the happiest and sunniest day of the year, he literally died for twenty-two minutes and he now balanced on a knife's edge. Oh yeah, and my mask, soaked in tears and blotched mascara, reminded me of that little ole' thing called COVID-19 that made the world turn crazy.

For days, Scott stayed in that coma, which meant he had minimal brain activity. It was awful enough to see him completely unconscious—but worse still to see half of his face buried behind a ventilator. But yet again, because of pandemic restrictions, I couldn't stay with him. So I agonized on the outside of the hospital wondering when he would wake up. Wondering if he would prove the doctors wrong. Wondering if he would smile at me and say, "What happened, my Kristi Love? Is Destiny's party over? When can we go home?"

I waited for normal—but normal never came.

PLEASE WAKE UP

Scott was in a coma for five days: June 21 through 26. In many ways this felt like a tomb experience. When Jesus died on the cross and was laid in the grave, the disciples must have thought everything was lost. Can you imagine what that was like?

They had bet everything on Jesus. They left their family businesses, their futures, and even their identities. Instead of fishermen, Peter, Andrew, James, and John were now "fishers of men." Instead of a tax collector, Matthew became a bearer of good news. Instead of a political radical (zealot), Simon's allegiance moved to Jesus. But now, everything they thought would happen was dashed on the rocks.

For three agonizing days, Jesus was dead. For me, I feared the worst for Scott. While his body was still alive, he was on a ventilator and failed his first spontaneous awakening trial. His doctors stopped the sedatives to see if his body would start breathing on its own. This is the first major test to get him off a ventilator. But his body wasn't ready. He was warm to the touch with fever, suffering from pneumonia, and his lungs weren't fully inflating because they were filled with vomit his body couldn't clear because he couldn't even cough.

Scott's heart was beating, but would *he* ever wake up? Would I get Scott back? The champion for the hurting, brilliant communicator, sold out man of God, wonderful daddy, and the man I had loved since middle school?

> **Scott's heart was beating, but would *he* ever wake up?**

GOING TO WAR

Not only was I (Scott) a trumpet player in the marching band, but at twelve years old, I was invited to join the prestigious Alabama School of Fine Arts. It was a special school for what they called "artistically gifted children." So I guess they thought I had some talent! But mostly, I think it was because I was fearless. I felt very comfortable performing on stage, almost like you feel when you come home after a long trip.

That feeling of *home* and *belonging* brings peace. And I found that peace acting, singing, and entertaining. However, this invitation meant I would have to change schools, and even life trajectories. It was a serious place about grooming the next generation of artists. But instead of telling me what to do, my parents said: "Scott, you have to make a decision. What do you think God wants you to do?"

I prayed about this possibility for several days before answering them.

"God said I could go if wanted, but that I am called to a greater purpose than performing."

Just like that, I didn't go. I stayed put. I pursued my calling to preach and have never looked back. Over the years, I have still acted in plays. Kristi and I always involved our children in fine arts (and, oh my, do we have some worship leaders in our family!).

Even though I didn't pursue performance, those days shaped me. Immersing myself in music–specifically worship music–taught me the Scriptures. It planted the seeds of God's Word into my heart. And even with my memory mostly getting wiped out, scripture and worship lyrics have come back more quickly than anything else.

As a kid, I would lay in bed at night and fall asleep listening to worship music. I've often been told I'm a lot like David, from the Bible. Worship was, and is, who I am. And I truly believe worship saved me.

A JERICHO MOMENT

I (Kristi) was stuck and felt powerless. But one thing I've learned over and over is that when you feel powerless, you need to run to the One who is always powerful. I had to get worship music into Scott's room. So I created a playlist on his phone with Bethel Music, Maverick City, and Daystar Worship. I included one special song written by our son Isaiah "Something's Chang ing" which seemed to be a prophetic song throughout this journey. We needed to shift the atmosphere around him. I knew he was there–and fundamentally, Scott is a worshiper.

After creating this playlist, I gave his phone to a doctor who attends our church. She is an absolute doll and could access Scott's room while I couldn't, due to the restrictions. She took his phone and extension cord, then set it right next to his bed. The music played on repeat almost continuously from then on.

This was a Jericho moment. Do you remember the story? Just like God's people, we had a battle to fight and a spiritual territory to conquer. The Book of Joshua shares the story: "Now the gates of Jericho were securely barred because of the Israel-ites. No one went out and no one came in" (Joshua 6:1). The city had a massive wall surrounding it, which archaeologists say is the oldest known protective wall in the world.[3] It stood twelve feet tall and six feet wide–and inside, a thirty-foot tower rose overlooking the city.

The Israelites were supposed to take this city. But the wall was impenetrable. It was too high, too wide, too strong. Sitting outside of the hospital, with its giant brick walls tow-ering above me, felt as daunting as their mission to conquer the unconquerable. Scott was inside, I was stuck outside. Scott was in a coma, and I had no idea what was going to happen when he woke up.

But let me tell you, I do know how to go to war just like the Israelites did. In fact, Scott is the one who taught me how to go to war in worship. Instead of going crazy in an all-out assault, God's people did something really weird. They marched around the city for a week. But the battle wasn't waged by warriors–it was waged by worshipers walking in the presence of God.

On the seventh day, they circled the city seven times. Then, it happened, the weapons of worship were unleashed: "When the trumpets sounded, the army shouted, and at the sound of the

---

[3]Ramos, Art. "Early Jericho." World History Encyclopedia. World History Encyclopedia, March 11, 2022. https://www.worldhistory.org/article/951/early-jericho/.

The battle wasn't waged by warriors—it was waged by worshipers walking in the presence of God.

trumpet, when the men gave a loud shout, the wall collapsed; so everyone charged straight in, and they took the city" (Joshua 6:20). I believe that our God fights our battles. I believed he would fight this one for us. And I knew deep into my bones that worship had to lead the way.

No kidding, just after our dear doctor friend took Scott's phone to his ICU room, a woman who had attended our church years before came walking around the corner. I was stunned to see her.

"Miss Delois, what are you doing here?" I asked.

"The Lord gave me a word for Scott and told me to come pray," she said.

I was overwhelmed with gratitude, because she had driven nearly three hours to do this.

"What's the word?" I asked.

"Reversal," she replied. And then she read Jeremiah 33:1-11, the Scripture God had given to her with the word.

This is what the Lord says: "You say about this place, 'It is a desolate waste, without people or animals.' Yet in the towns of Judah and the streets of Jerusalem that are deserted, inhabited by neither people nor animals, there will be heard once more the sounds of joy and gladness, the voices of bride and bride-groom, and the voices of those who bring thank offerings to the house of the Lord, saying, 'Give thanks to the Lord Almighty, for the Lord is good; his love endures forever.' For I will restore the fortunes of the land as they were before," says the Lord.

There was the promise: God was going to reverse deso-lation into restored fortunes. His promises and plans over our life were going to be fulfilled. And I knew this season would lead to breakthrough, restoration, and revival for many. This was such an encouragement. And honestly, this was the breath of fresh air I so desperately needed while Scott fought for every breath.

THE STONE STARTS TO ROLL

The next day was Destiny's *very* delayed high school graduation ceremony. We tried to be as happy as we could given the circumstances. But it was wonderful to have a somewhat normal experience. To see Destiny with her best friends in that light blue gown, cap, and honor student ribbons was a joy.

We were eating lunch before our outdoor ceremony when I received a call from Pastor David. Honestly, I wasn't answering calls at this point because I was too overwhelmed. I only picked up if it was the hospital, family, or David or Cindy.

"Hey David, what's up?"

"Kristi, you better call the hospital. They called the church offices looking for you. They said they need to talk to you right away," he said.

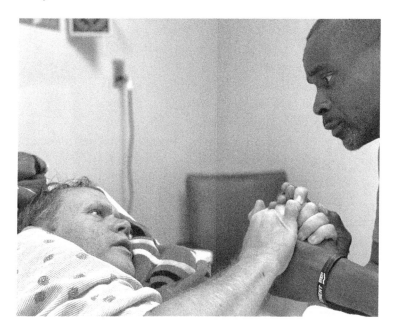

My stomach dropped. I hung up and Destiny and I ran outside to call the hospital. For some reason, they had our church number for my contact information, and our lay pastor who answered started freaking out because she couldn't get a hold of me. She now feared the worst for Scott *and* for me. Good grief!

I reached the nurse and she walked me through what was going on. She updated me with the laundry list of medications and equipment they had him on. All the while I'm having a panic attack waiting for her to say the word ... *but* ...

... we tried *but* your husband had another heart attack.

... we did everything we could *but* your husband's pneumonia is worse than we thought.

...we did everything we could *but* your husband isn't going to wake up.

Instead of a *but*, though, I heard this: "Oh, by the way, Scott squeezed my hand this morning."

"What?" Destiny and I pretty much shouted.

"I was holding his hand while we were prepping to remove his ventilator. I just said, 'Scott, can you squeeze my hand? Then he did."

"Are you serious? You're not lying to me?"

I was so stunned I could hardly believe it.

"I'm serious, he squeezed my hand!" she said.

"So he can hear you? He can understand?"

"Apparently so," she replied.

Destiny and I collapsed into each other's arms, and she said, "Mom, he's gonna be okay."

I believed her.

This was a huge day. We found joy and hope for the first time in five days. The tombstone was starting to roll away. We still didn't get to see him, but at least we knew that somehow, some way, he was still there. We received multiple prophetic words, dreams, and visions of hope during these first few days. They strengthened us when we felt too exhausted to stand.

> **But then, like another little miracle, he smiled at me.**

ANOTHER LITTLE MIRACLE

The next morning wasn't filled with sunshine and rainbows, and it was just like the enemy to launch every attack imaginable, all to break your faith with fear. They called me (and not the church offices, thank God!) and said he'd begun having stroke-like symptoms early that morning. They needed to check him for brain swelling and, of course, gave me an update of all of the crazy stuff he was on. However, because they had his phone, the nurse asked, "Do you want to FaceTime with him to see how he's doing?"

Yes! Of course I did.

Tears came the moment I saw him. He was pale, his face covered in stubble. He couldn't speak, so the only reply I got to my "hey babe" and "I love you" was the unsettling background noise of a tense hospital room. But then, like another little miracle, he smiled at me. The last two years of our lives have been filled with a million little miracles.

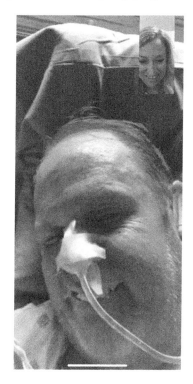

I couldn't believe it! But that's when I knew for sure, he was still there. He'd woken up. We made it through five dark days. Now we could finally start figuring out what was happening with his mind. So far, all we had was a hand squeeze and a smile. But for now, that was enough. I pushed fear as far away as I could and held tight to God's promises.

Chapter 8

CLIMBING MOUNT RECOVERY

I (Kristi) went to church on Sunday, June 28th. It was seven days into this terrifying experience. We still didn't know what to expect. Scott seemed to be responding to the worship music, but he still didn't have a handle on where he was, who he was, or anything else.

Now, I could have easily chosen to stay home from church that Sunday morning. Everyone would've understood why I would want some space. However, I know the importance of being in God's presence–even more so today. He is my lifeline! And I wanted to be surrounded by the people I knew prayed nonstop for us.

Isolating myself would have been like Lazarus staying in the tomb, Job burying himself further in a pit of misery, or Ruth leaving Naomi to return to her people. Going to church was my way to step out of the tomb, climb out of the pit, and stay near God's people and stay in *His* presence.

The church service was refreshing. The worship was powerful. The people were beautifully kind, caring, and supportive. But every inch of our church building reminded me of Scott. We had prayed over every chair in the sanctuary together hundreds of times. We had lifted our hands in worship together thousands of times. And we had done life with these people for years.

While it was a special time, it was also painful. So as I said goodbye and left the building, wiping tears away, my phone rang. It was one of Scott's doctors who said, "Kristi, you'd better get down here. Scott is awake, but very agitated. We need help calming him down."

I rushed straight to the hospital, practically sprinting to the metal elevator doors. It felt like an eternity to rumble up to the ICU. When the doors slid open, I burst out and found Scott's room. But then, with my hand on the handle, I froze. I was scared to open the door because I didn't know what (or who) I would find on the other side. But my fear was met with an abiding peace, the Holy Spirit, who saw me not just through the doorway, but even to writing these words right now. However, that didn't mean the sight on the other side of the door was pretty.

Honestly, I don't know what else I expected. But seeing him upset and confused crushed me. Squeezing the nurse's hand, trying to lift his head, and that brief smile he gave me on FaceTime had gotten my hopes up. But seeing him now, for the first time in nearly a week, shook me. The reality of how severe his condition was smacked me in the face.

> **I didn't even know how to talk to my husband, let alone comprehend the trauma to his body and mind.**

I didn't even know how to talk to my husband, let alone comprehend the trauma to his body and mind.

I spent the next four days holding his hands down. My job was to keep him from ripping out the tubes and wires that he still needed. They eventually covered his hands with padded mittens to keep him from hurting himself or removing the equipment.

I talked gently to him, trying to reassure him while the worship music played. I had no idea if he could understand me, but I hoped something inside of him remembered my voice. *Remember me, remember me, remember me,* my heart begged.

It felt like we were at the base of an impossibly tall mountain. Sheer cliffs dropped thousands of feet into dark valleys.

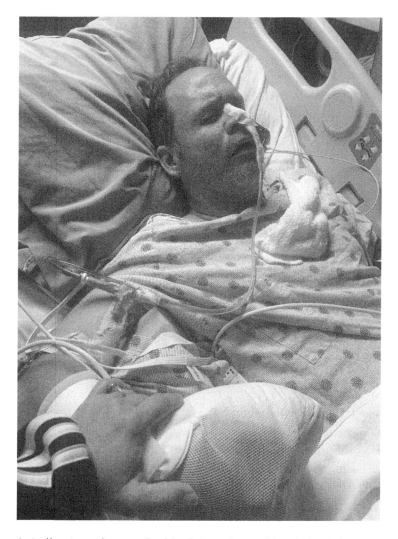

Spindly pinnacles reached high into the air like skeletal fingers. Every step toward the summit just reminded me how far we had to climb.

Then, on June 30th, after I had been in his ICU room for forty-eight hours, Scott finally spoke. We caught a glimmer that his mind was working. He was piecing together who he was and what had happened. But it was one of the most heartbreaking moments of my life.

"MY MOM . . . ?"

As we've explained, Scott and his mom were close. He loved her dearly. Losing her was one of the most painful things that had ever happened to him—and given some of the pain we have faced in life and ministry, that is saying a *lot*. It only makes sense that now, less than two months later, that searing pain resurfaced.

Scott was mumbling, whispering something quietly. I leaned in to hear what he was trying to say.

"What, baby?" I asked softly. Again, getting my hopes up.

His eyes opened just a crack and he focused on me for the first time. Then I saw sorrow spill across his face.

"My mom dead . . . ?" he asked.

"Yes, honey. I'm so sorry," I said, tears tracing their well-worn path down my cheeks.

This began an infinite loop of Scott forgetting, and then reliving, his mother's death. Watching anyone go through this is heartbreaking. But watching your husband suffer one of his most traumatic events over and over is soul crushing.

Then he would drift back into his semi-unconscious state. Groaning. Agitated. Trying to pull the mitts off. You could see him trying to understand what was happening—but his mind simply couldn't grasp it.

Still, the worship music played. The doctors, nurses, and physical therapists all remarked on what a powerful presence they felt in our room. Saying that walking into the other patients' rooms, with no sound except for beeping machines, made them want to bring the worship music to them. They told us that people needed this. And that was easy for me to understand, because we needed this and we knew the power of worship.

Throughout this first week, the nurses asked me to give him small commands like this to see if he could process them and follow the directions.

"Snap your fingers, Scott," I said.

To our surprise, he snapped his fingers the very first time! So I asked him again . . . and again . . . and again . . . but nothing more happened. I spent the rest of the day encouraging him to follow small tasks and directions–or to say even one word. But a weak snap of his fingers is all that we could accomplish. It was something, but it certainly wasn't feeling like enough.

THERE IN A SNAP

About three years ago, Scott and I were at an event for our health coaching business. There were hundreds of other coaches gathered to learn and grow together. After a day of mind-blowing sessions, we had all finished eating supper and were hanging out around a beautiful pool. Stars twinkled overhead and conversations were in full swing. We were surrounded by the most inspiring, engaging people we've ever met. But while I was chatting away, Scott was laser-focused on someone across the pool from us.

"What are you looking at, Scott?" I asked.

"You see that couple?" he said, pointing. I followed his gaze and picked out the husband and wife he was pointing at.

"God gave me a message for them, and we need to go share it," Scott said.

"Okay, well let's definitely find them later tonight and connect. That will mean a lot to them, I'm sure," I suggested.

"We need to go right now," Scott said.

I tilted my head, excused us from the conversation, and we wound our way through the crowd.

While we were familiar with the couple, we had never had a substantive conversation with Russ and Traci Scarce. They were connected to Scott's brother, Pat, fellow health coaches, and loved Jesus. But that's about all we knew!

We walked up to Traci, the most animated, fiery blonde woman you can imagine!

"Hi Traci," I said. "I know this is super random, but Scott has a word for you and Russ."

Traci looked surprised. But she called Russ out from the pool. He pushed his way onto the concrete, walked over soaking wet, and greeted us with a smile, obviously wondering what this was about.

Even though we were surrounded by hundreds of people, it suddenly felt like we were the only people there.

Scott said, "God's got some words for you that I believe He wants me to share. Are you open?"

Russ and Traci looked at each other. Then Russ replied, "Absolutely–bring it!"

For the next five minutes, I watched Scott share things about Russ's life that *no one* but he and Traci knew. He spoke to specific situations, hardships, and strife that Russ had been through. My jaw dropped as I listened, because Russ's life had been *hard*. Like really, really hard. Then, Scott told him the exact number of years a particularly difficult season had been. Russ and Traci were in disbelief. And then Scott said, "Those are the years the locusts took away."

It was almost like Scott had an earpiece God was whispering into. He continued, speaking life and God's love over Russ. Encouraging him *and* reassuring him of God's huge master plan for his life that was just beginning to unfold. We shared a teary, intimate moment together at that party–and none of us will ever forget it. Today, Russ and Traci are some of our closest, dearest friends (prophesying will do that!). Recently, Russ shared with us that it was the first time this had ever happened to him, and it created an instant bond between us.

That's why, after spending a week of nearly sleepless nights in the ICU with Scott, I received a text message from Traci that may have saved me. She and Russ were desperate to know what was going on, and she had called several times. However, each time my phone rang, I couldn't answer. Either I was actively caring for Scott and literally couldn't speak, or I was too overwhelmed.

In the hours before her message, I was hurtling toward rock bottom. I couldn't stop thinking, "I just need to die ... I can't do this ..."

I didn't know what Scott's progression would be. Would he recover? Would he worsen? Would he be admitted into a facility for the rest of his life? Imagining visiting him with our kids, seeing him stuck in a wheelchair, and living by himself in a room was horrifying. But I had no way of predicting what our future held. All I could do was desperately pray for strength to endure until we had answers, healing, or both.

Then my phone screen lit up with Traci's text.

Traci: I know Pat asked us not to bombard you with texts. But we can't handle this. How are you?
Me: I'm doing so bad I can't even talk right now.
Traci: Can I call?

I thought for a moment, unsure if I could handle the conversation. But I knew I couldn't do this alone.

Me: Yes.

My phone started buzzing immediately. Scott was sleeping, so I snuck out of the room.

"Hi Traci," I answered.

She cut right to it: "Can Russ come? Will they let him in the room?"

Relief flooded my body. I told Traci yes and explained the uncanny timing of her call. Just fifteen minutes before this question the nurse manager told me, "You need to go home, you're exhausted. You can find someone to swap out with you as long as there's only one person in the room."

Within minutes of hanging up, she texted: "Russ's flight is booked. He'll be there tomorrow night."

For the first time in a week, I had back up. I'm so grateful Traci listened to the prompting of the Holy Spirit to text one more time and ask for the call. If she hadn't, I don't know what would've happened. Thankfully, we never had to find out.

At 6:00 p.m. the next day Russ walked into our room. I could see he was shocked at seeing Scott's state. However, he held it together and hugged me. Then, I debriefed him and made the extremely hard decision to leave and rest.

Russ stayed through the night until 9:00 the next morning. I didn't realize how exhausted I really was until I went home and slept in my own bed. While my world had shrunk to Scott's hospital room, the world had kept moving ahead. I was overwhelmed and felt insanely behind in everything. But thankfully we had incredible coaching partners in our business, amazing leaders at Daystar, and strong children who each stepped up for us all.

The next morning Russ explained that, at first, he had no idea what to do for Scott. All he could do was pray. Then, the Lord told him, "Play his music." And it calmed Scott enough to sleep.

Russ was at the hospital for five days and this was the routine every night. The second night, he told me Scott started nodding his head to the beat, ever so slightly. The third night, he began to move his lips to some of the lyrics. The fourth night, he mumbled some of the words out loud! This was such a breakthrough Russ called the nurse in to show her.

Unbelievably, Scott pointed at her when she came in and spoke, "Girl, you are anointed."

Both she and Russ were stunned. This was the first full sentence he'd spoken. And it was complex and loaded with meaning. After she left the room, Scott told Russ, "That girl will be worshiping with us before she leaves."

Then, he faded back into his semi-conscious state.

I believe Scott's healing began with worship. When the doctors told us he would never speak again, worship started to return his words. When the doctors said he'd never regain his mind, worship awoke his prophetic spirit. When the doctors said he'd never be the same, the loving man we knew began to re-emerge.

Hours later, Russ left to use the bathroom as some of the nursing staff came in to check his vitals. Five minutes later he walked back into the room to a scene that blew his mind.

*Unbelievably, Scott pointed
at her when she came in and
spoke, "Girl, you are anointed."*

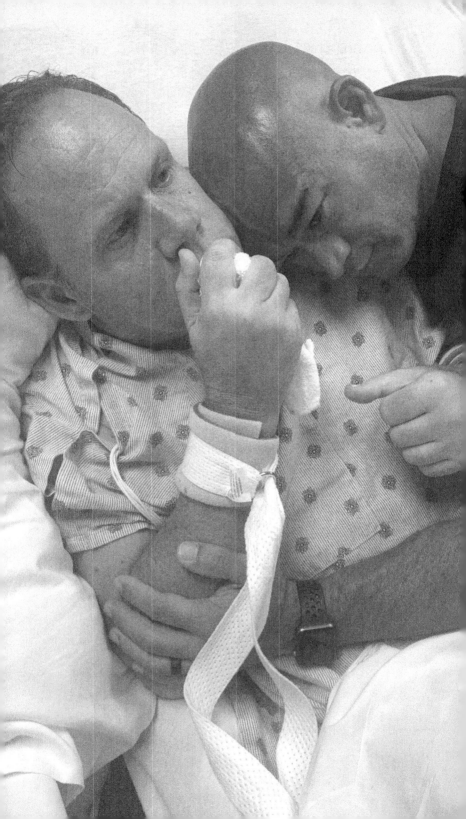

There was that same nurse, kneeling at the side of Scott's bed, holding his hand, and singing "Raise a Hallelujah" with Scott.

Russ knew his friend, mentor, and spiritual father was still there. And to this day, he'll call Scott just to say hi because, as he told me, "I trust God still has an earpiece in Scott's ear like the first time we met. So when I need it, he'll speak words of life and wisdom to me through that man."

In total, Russ took the night shift with Scott for a week and Pastor David covered the early morning hours until I could arrive, allowing me to rest at home and do what little catching up I could. It's difficult to express how crucial his and Traci's support were for us. Their love is humbling. Their friendship is invaluable. And our love for them is eternal. Especially because I needed every stitch of rest I could get for the journey ahead.

THE LONG CLIMB AHEAD

Every mountain simply revealed another one twice as tall behind it. Scott couldn't speak. He couldn't recognize most of us. And though we'd catch glimpses of him, we didn't know if he would ever return.

Would I get my husband back?

Would my kids get their daddy back?

Would our church get their pastor back?

Would anyone get their friend back?

Most of all, would Scott get all of us back?

I resolved to not lose hope. I declared that this crisis didn't cancel our purpose. However, the doubts lurked beneath the surface. Russ and Traci's support had come just as I hit the breaking point. But I was still teetering on the edge of the abyss.

The reality that we may have lost who Scott used to be for-ever hurt deeply. But the thought that he would never reclaim his brilliant, capable, caring, and passionate self hurt even worse. It was only as he started therapy that we began to see the full extent of the long climb that lay ahead of us.

Chapter 9

SOME THINGS YOU NEED TO FORGET

I'll *(Scott) be honest, I don't remember much of anything that Kristi has shared in the last few chapters.* It's either a blur or a blank spot. It's like part of my life got deleted. Like a computer that got reset, losing a bunch of files in the process. But overtime, some parts came back. It's like getting a new phone; you have to re-download your apps. But for a long time, you stare at a little faded icon that fills in with color as it finishes installing. That was like my brain.

But now, I'm okay with the memories that haven't come back. Sometimes you need to forget some things. Especially the bad things. Because we get stuck in cycles of focusing on what's wrong. This steals our attention from meditating on what's right. This is a path of pain. It keeps people stuck in the past.

> I've learned that a crisis doesn't cancel your purpose, it reveals it.

I've learned that a crisis doesn't cancel your purpose, it reveals it. Hard times show you who you are. And because I'm still a preacher, I think the Bible explains it best in Proverbs 17:3: "The crucible for silver and the furnace for gold, but the LORD tests the heart." Precious metals are superheated to remove the junk. This is how they make "pure gold." God does the same to our hearts. But that heat isn't very comfortable.

I hated it. I still hate it sometimes. It's a terrible feeling to know what you're capable of but can't seem to do. Sometimes Kristi and I would watch old videos of me preaching. I knew I was watching me—but it wasn't *me* anymore. I was scared that guy died and would never come back.

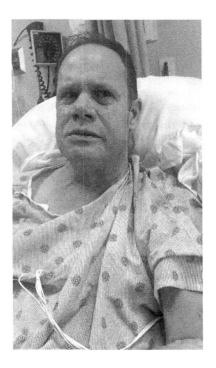

I don't remember this, but Kristi took a video of me on July 6, 2020, about three weeks after my cardiac arrest. I had regained very little speech at this point. Tears streamed down my face as we listened to worship music. Kristi asked me why I was crying. I whispered, "That's what I used to do. That's why I'm crying."

I was a worship leader. I was a pastor. My doctorate diploma still hangs on my office wall. So I *know* I'm Dr. Scott Schatzline. But the bits and pieces of my early recovery are mostly feelings of confusion, sadness, anger, and helplessness. To this day, it's hard for me to compliment or say good things about myself, even though Kristi says, "You're all that and a bag of chips!"

Your situation might not be like mine. But you still have to deal with hard things. Some of you are in the middle of that "hard" right now. You might have sunk into a valley and can't imagine a way out. In the last year, I've met many hurting people who want to give up on life altogether. Some in person. Others in online groups. But my message is the same: "Don't give up. This world needs you. You are loved." The only path out of the valley is love.

Loving God. Loving others. Loving yourself. Remembering who you are while forgetting some of the bad things that happened. My life is still about the same thing: loving people like there is no tomorrow.

FIGHT FOR WHAT'S RIGHT FOR YOU

It hurt to watch my (Kristi) husband hurt. His speech slowly returned in the first few weeks after the heart attack and brain injury. Not fully. But enough to where we could communicate. He still didn't understand—or even remember—that something had happened. No exaggeration, we had to have this conversation at least twenty-fives times per day. He also strained to remember the names for common things like cups, pens, and shoes.

The day after he cried while remembering he was a worship leader, our daughter Destiny came to visit him. He didn't recognize her. He was kind and interested in her life. And even prayed for her. He still didn't realize who she was. But the one thing he did not forget was music, so Destiny began to sing worship with her dad.

Scott looked at me and said, "She reminds me of my wife."

Meanwhile, the hospital staff kept working with him. He did simple physical therapy routines like matching his right hand to the therapist's right hand and walking just a few steps to the room door and back to his bed. That's as far as he could go. It was too risky to let him walk out of the room; one reason was COVID, and the other reason was we might not get him back to the room. This man was ready to go!

So much so, that one morning he pulled off his gown and started dancing with the nurse on duty–stark naked!

"Scott Schatzline," I said, "You can't do that!"

"It's okay, I got him," she said. She was sweet, calm, and understanding. We laughed, got Scott situated back in his bed, and marked that down as one of the happy moments in a string of extremely difficult ones.

Happy moments like the times Pastor David had to trick Scott into eating his medicine-filled chocolate pudding. Or when Julian spent hours playing worship songs and singing as Scott pretended to direct the choir like he used to. Or when our friend and Scott's barber, Eddie, came to give him a nice trim, shave, and a haircut.

Meanwhile, even though his therapists were trying so hard and caring for him well, Scott's progress was painfully slow– too slow. I knew he needed specialized care. I felt like they were treating him like a normal case when, in reality, his trauma was severe. To be honest, I don't think anyone knew the gravity of what we were really facing. And his window of recovery was rapidly closing.

So I pushed our first case manager to transfer us to a facility I believed would be more capable of helping Scott. But she kept pushing back, saying, "He's not qualified to go there. So far, he hasn't met the requirements."

This stunned me. Isn't that *why* you go to rehab in the first place? Why on Earth would someone need to meet higher standards to get into intensive, specialized therapy? So I kept pushing. And she continued to return excuses.

"They don't have enough beds."

"No one gives me answers when I call."

"I've sent in his paperwork but haven't heard back."

Nothing she said rang true to me. I knew we needed to be somewhere with more capability and, frankly, that was just more comfortable. We obviously had a long road ahead of us. Cramped in a small hospital room with nothing but hospital food and stale coffee added even more friction to the sandpaper of our situation. And in the constant bustle, Scott wasn't getting the rest he needed.

I had fire in my bones. I've always been the kind of person who doesn't take no for an answer and believes where there's a will, there's a way. This is when I learned unequivocally: *you can't count on anyone to advocate for you.* Sad as it sounds, I began to assume people didn't follow through on their promises. And unfortunately, I had this assumption proven to me a hundred times over.

It was obvious to me our case manager wasn't really going to fight for us to get into the proper facility. So I contacted them myself and was put in touch with our case manager's counterpart at the specialized rehab center. She told me that she hadn't received a single call, gotten a page of paperwork, or even heard the name Scott Schatzline.

Just what I thought.

If you ever care for a loved one in the hospital, take this advice: fight tooth and nail for what you know is right, because no one else will fight for you. Always take matters into your own hands. Follow up with the people who are supposed to be handling things. Push. Email. Call. Drop by. Remember, the squeaky wheel gets the grease. And the grease may just save someone's life.

And guess what happened? Within an hour of speaking with this new case manager we learned that Scott qualified for a transfer, and they just needed some documentation. To put it lightly, our first case manager was unhappy about this! I think she felt called out because it was obvious she had done nothing she said she had. She got rude and petty. But do you know what? My husband was going to receive the care he was supposed to.

Of course, there were hiccups in the transfer. Our first case manager had also failed to secure Scott what's called a LifeVest. It's a wearable defibrillator that snugs against his skin, like body armor for his heart. The vest corrects any abnormal heart rhythms with minor electric shocks. However, the transfer wasn't going to get approved without one–even though he was supposed to have had one by now.

I frantically broadcast on social media that we needed a connection to someone who worked for the vest company itself. And wouldn't you know, someone in our church just happened to be one of their local reps! God showed up for us again. So we were able to fast-track Scott's vest in just a few days. And in less than a week from my first call, we finally arrived at the new treatment center.

LEMME GET YOUR DIGITS

They took Scott to the rehab center in an ambulance. I followed as closely as I could but had to park in a different place (and pay $25 to park there for less than five minutes!). I jogged around the building to the entrance the ambulance had pulled up to as they were wheeling Scott into the front doors. And like a little kid on Christmas morning, Scott was all smiles!

I caught up to them and he said, "Hey baby girl, what's your name!"

We all laughed. Everyone knew this was a victory. And we really needed one.

But as we piled into the elevator, Scott wouldn't stop.

"Girl, lemme get your digits! Put your digits into my phone. Lemme get 'em!"

We walked into his new room, still smiling at Scott's flirtiness and charm. And while it was the smallest room they had, it was a room at the right place. However, as soon as the staff left, Scott got upset and asked, "Why are we in the hospital? I thought we were going home?"

So it began again. I had to explain to him what happened. *Why we had moved from the old hospital to a new one ... That he needed more treatment ... What was going to happen in this new place ...* It was like this every day. An endless loop of forgetting, explaining, sadness, repeat.

The rehab center was connected to the larger hospital, which had restaurants, a walking bridge, and our Holy Grail: Starbucks! A couple of days later I left him for the first time to get supper at the restaurant inside of the hospital. I was gone for barely twenty minutes. But by the time I came back with supper, he was beside himself. Confused as to why he was there. Angry that I abandoned him. He pulled off all of his monitors, LifeVest, everything–trying to run away. Then he refused to talk to me for a few hours.

The consolation was that Scott was finally sleeping through the night. And I laid right beside him in a reclining chair. However, while he slept, I wept. I had reached a breaking point. We were an hour away from our family and friends. I felt so lonely and isolated and desperate. My whole life was flipped upside down–and the only time I could actually reflect on our new reality was in the middle of the night, because Scott still required my total attention at every waking moment.

> However, while he slept, I wept. I had reached a breaking point.

The truth was, I was *dying* on the inside. I thought there was no way I could do this anymore. How long will I have to do this? When will this nightmare end? I cried through dark thoughts. Sometimes, for the briefest of moments, I even imagined what it would feel like to walk away.

But I'd immediately shake myself out of this place and whisper, "Holy Ghost, you've got to help me . . ." He did. During those nights I felt like I was hooked up to supernatural life support.

One night I cried, begging God for a "suddenly" blessing, and a new nurse slipped in quietly and saw me shivering beneath the thin blanket on that stiff chair, makeup running down my face, and guess what her name was?

She introduced herself: "I'm Scott's nurse for the night. My name is Blessing. Let's get you taken care of."

Blessing also brought me sheets, a pillow, and a warmer blanket, helping me get situated. She cared for me like a mama—and I desperately needed it at that moment. I have found that whenever we needed help most, we got it. Even her name was a confirmation that God was with us.

When I was unraveling at the first hospital, Russ came ... When Scott's case was falling through the cracks, a new case manager helped ... When we needed a vest, a church member swooped in at the eleventh hour ... When I was broken, shivering, and alone, my mind swirling with dark thoughts, Scott's nurse Blessing cared for me ... When I was weak (like every ten seconds), God was strong and taught me what it means to pray without ceasing ...

You've probably seen the old poster of the footprints in the sand. You may have even thought it was as corny as I did after seeing it for the thousandth time! But my goodness if it's not the perfect illustration of how I felt. If you've never seen it, it goes like this:[4]

One night I dreamed a dream.
As I was walking along the beach with my Lord.
Across the dark sky flashed scenes from my life.
For each scene, I noticed two sets of footprints in the sand,
One belonging to me and one to my Lord.

After the last scene of my life flashed before me,
I looked back at the footprints in the sand.
I noticed that at many times along the path of my life,
especially at the very lowest and saddest times,
there was only one set of footprints.

This really troubled me, so I asked the Lord about it.
"Lord, you said once I decided to follow you,
You'd walk with me all the way.

---

[4]The exact author is in dispute, but the message is powerful all the same!

*But I noticed that during the saddest and most troublesome
times of my life,
there was only one set of footprints.
I don't understand why, when I needed You the most, You
would leave me."*

*He whispered, "My precious child, I love you and will
never leave you
Never, ever, during your trials and testings.
When you saw only one set of footprints,
It was then that I carried you."*

Today, nearly two years removed from these events, I don't know if I could go through this again. In fact, I know I couldn't do it on my own strength. God carried me. He carried us. It's hard to describe the 360-degree exhaustion for Scott, for me, and for our family.

Every ten minutes I had to remind him of everything we'd just talked about because his short-term memory was gone. He would get stuck in loops, repeating the same things non-stop. Worst of all was when he had to relive both his sister Reneé's passing and his mother's death. So much pain. Like a wound being bandaged, only to be ripped off and split open again and again. But through it all, like the old Andraé Crouch song would say, "I've learned to trust in Jesus, I've learned to trust in God."

God didn't only comfort us with His Spirit, He also brought amazing people into our lives.

I'm so grateful for every caregiver. The speech therapists, occupational therapists, music therapists, and everyone in between. They brought moments of humor and joy, as well as comfort and peace. While we had rough patches (as I've described), almost everyone in our daily rehabilitation had hearts to heal, help, and give hope. And we needed it. Because I knew, if I could just make it to 6 o'clock every night, we had navigated another day on the stormy seas.

Every night we had two hours of worship time together. Our room turned into a sanctuary. The music bathed us in strength. And it brought peace to Scott's mind. This was very important and life-giving and became a non-negotiable. Because this is how Scott began to sleep through the night. After two hours in God's presence, he was asleep and finally getting the rest his body needed.

"IS IT MY BIRFDAY?"

We stayed at the rehab facility for twelve days. So by the day it was time for us to discharge and go home, Scott was just over a month post-cardiac arrest. I was both excited *and* terrified to go home. Excited because we could gain some semblance of normalcy. Sleeping in our bed with our pillows and sheets that didn't smell industrially cleaned. Cooking food in our kitchen. Establishing new routines. However, I was scared because Scott still was in no shape to be left alone.

How would I do things as simple as showering and trust he wouldn't walk outside and get lost? (Which did happen, by the way.) What if something went wrong and he needed emergency medical attention? How long would I have to do this? When would Scott snap out of it? Most of all, was I really up to the task?

Then, the night before we went home Scott started saying, "I feel good ... I feel great ... I feel wonderful ..." He was quoting Bill Murray's lines from *What About Bob?*, one of his favorite movies! So I said, "You know what, baby? We're going to have a date tonight!"

We went to "dinner" at the vending machine down the hallway, buying some popcorn and peanut M&Ms. Then, we snuggled up and watched *What About Bob?* It was a promising end to our time here. I felt safe here, but it was time for the baby birds to leave the nest for the next stages of recovery (whatever it would look like).

Just before discharge day, our kids, and Scott's dad came to lunch with us in the connected restaurant. It was so nice to be together–especially because COVID restrictions had so limited visitors we'd yet to enjoy each other's company all at once.

It felt so good to walk into our house together just a couple days later. I hoped the familiar furniture and smell and rooms would jumpstart his memory. But his first words were: "Whose house is this?"

I guess it was going to be awhile until he knew what home meant. Or even remembered all of the wonderful things that had happened here. However, one bit of childlike excitement returned: it was about a week until his forty-ninth birthday! And just like a little kid, he couldn't wait.

At first, it was adorable. Like a little kid, he would ask, "Is it my birfday?"

But then he'd get stuck in a loop and ask every ten minutes. Literally. Every ten minutes (on the minute) for a week. It was sweet, but exhausting to help him understand.

His birthday finally arrived on Sunday, August 2nd. It was also our first time back in church. Everyone was elated to see him. And again, I hoped the familiar faces and the church build-ing would trigger deeper memories. Daystar was a fundamental part of us. Even though he didn't remember anyone, he most certainly remembered how to worship. And that Sunday, he danced and praised so hard King David himself wouldn't have kept up. However, he worshiped so hard he set his LifeVest off! After resetting it and getting situated, Pastors David and Cindy, and Scott's dad, Bishop Schatzline, invited us onto the stage to share.

I don't remember exactly what I said. Probably many tearful thank yous for the prayers, help, and faithfulness of the people. It was an emotional moment without a dry eye in the place. Then, for the first time in over a month, we handed Scott a microphone. And I'll tell you what, *no one* forgets what he said that day.

"Church starts at home," Scott said. "What we do on Sundays should just be a confirmation of what you've already been doing at home!"

This shocked us because he had *no idea* about the pandemic, restrictions, shutdowns, or any of the people forced into having church in their own living rooms. His words had a meaning beyond what he could have known. And then, Scott built on his momentum—in a surprising way.

He continued, "Husbands and wives, listen to me: if you're not sexy toward your spouse, you'll be sexy toward someone you shouldn't be! So go home and have lots of sex. That is good!"

The congregation went from shared tears to uproarious laughter. Pastor David, Pastor Cindy, and I were cracking up on stage. It was hilarious, but honestly so true. Scott had no filter. But his heart as a spiritual father, pastoral wisdom, and preacher's fire were still there. It was a good morning that got even better when we arrived home.

Our dear friends Wayne and Courtney Pendle were back for the first time since the cardiac arrest. Scott's brother Pat and a few of our very close friends were also over. We had a small party and were able to tell Scott: "Yes! It is your birfday!"

We laughed and reminisced. And of course, Pat couldn't keep himself from being a big brother. He convinced Scott that he'd given him his car as a birthday present to *him*! Those two can't keep from messing with each other. This too brought a small sense of normalcy. But after everyone went home, it was just us, just me, just the nagging question, *Kristi, can you really do this?*

I still didn't know the answer.

WONDER WOMAN

If you are in that hard place, like I (Scott) have been, there are three things I need you to do.

First, tell me that you're not going to quit. Quitting, ending things, or staying stuck in your pain is Devil talk. Keep going. Breakthrough is coming. And even though that sounds clichéd, I can tell you it's real. Now, your life may never look the same. Some things may not be restored exactly as they were. But it's not over. If you are breathing, God is not done with you!

Second, look at the people who have stuck with you and appreciate them. I'm not alone in calling my Kristi Love Wonder Woman! That is no joke. Her dedication to me has been super-hero level. Even as we write this book together, and I hear some of the hard things she went through for the first time, I'm in awe at how amazing she is. She inspires me. I love her more than I ever have before.

Third, surround yourself with the right voices. If you listen to the right voices, you can make the right choices. Only take phone calls from the right people. Stop following negative people on social media. Fill your mind and spirit with positivity and truth. Truth about who God is. Truth about who you are. Truth about your ability to overcome.

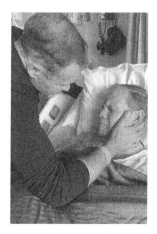
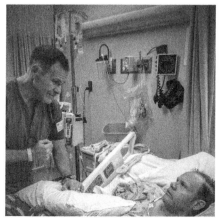

If you are breathing,
God is not done with you!

Right voices, right choices. Remember *The Little Mermaid*? When did things start going wrong for her? When she started listening to Ursula. Wrong voices, wrong choices!

You don't have room for Ursulas who never speak life into you. I'll lay it out for you like this. Show me your friends, I'll show you your future. Boom. That's it.

Remember Job and his two "friends," Eliphaz and Bildad? Job had lost everything. So both of these guys assumed it was because Job had majorly sinned. Obviously his misfortune had to be a punishment, right? However, as we all know, Job was blameless—he was a target of spiritual attack from Satan. But Eliphaz and Bildad didn't want to hear it and kept speaking poison to Job. Finally, he got fed up with them and said in Job 16:1-5 (MSG):

> "I've had all I can take of your talk.
> What a bunch of miserable comforters!
> Is there no end to your windbag speeches?
> What's your problem that you go on and on like this?
> If you were in my shoes,
> I could talk just like you.
> I could put together a terrific tirade
> and really let you have it.
> But I'd never do that. I'd console and comfort,
> make things better, not worse!"

Do you know that one of the hardest things about these last two years hasn't just been my brain injury or medical stays? It's been the negativity from some people who were supposed to be our closest friends. Instead of encouragement, we got discouragement. It killed us on the inside. It even had an impact on our children—especially our son, Isaiah.

He is fiercely loyal, especially to his daddy. And during my recovery, a person in our life decided to start spreading rumors that my cardiac arrest was from the health and wellness program we coach. Obviously, this couldn't have been further from the truth, because, as previously mentioned, my cardiologist confirmed it literally saved my life. Had I not gotten physically healthy, and lost eighty pounds, I would be dead.

Even though ministry families (and their kids in particular) know how to roll with the gossip, lies, and mean-spiritedness, this crossed a line for Isaiah. He immediately jumped to my defense, directly addressing the individual and confronting the lie. I was so proud of him for following Jesus's direction for resolving conflict in Matthew 18:15, "If your brother or sister sins, go and point out their fault, just between the two of you. If they listen to you, you have won them over."

Like Job, we had to cut people like this out of our lives for a season. And I want you to know it's okay—and even necessary—to be very careful about whose voices you listen to. And who you let have a seat at your table, especially when you're in hard seasons. The enemy whispers enough lies and launches too many attacks as it is for you to be beaten down by people who are supposed to have your back. However, in the midst of our mess, trials, and stupid stuff, God's love never quits. Kristi showed me that kind of love continually. From the day I died to this very moment.

That love constantly reminded me of God's Father heart toward us. His unending love chases us to the ends of the Earth and back. And one memory that resurfaced was a number of years ago when I had to walk in that same pursuing love.

Our son Noah was in the middle of an extremely difficult season. Every day was a battle for his life and identity. The hardest part for us was that he moved to Miami and was going through much of it alone. One day, while praying for him through tears, I heard the Holy Spirit say, "Scott, drop everything and go to him."

As a pastor, though, this was difficult. We had a million things happening at the church, plus I would have to abruptly leave and miss a Sunday service where I was preaching. How could I skip out at the last minute? But pastors and ministry leaders, hear me on this: your first ministry is your family, not your flock!

Kristi and I had always worked hard to do this, balancing family life and ministry. We never missed a play, a game, or a family night. Still, we nearly lost one of our sons. I knew my choice would define our family, legacy, and ministry forever. Kristi and I weren't going to sacrifice our kids on the altar of ministry. So, I bought a plane ticket without saying a word to Noah, and I showed up on his doorstep.

He was shocked to see me, but relieved when he realized I wasn't there to judge him or chew him out for his decisions. I was just there to be his dad and love him. And I believe me leaving to be with him in a busy ministry season (and especially missing a Sunday unplanned) spoke volumes to him. It said, "Your daddy loves you more than ministry, more than anything in the world."

Do you know that God's heart is just like that toward us? He always values people over projects. Before anything else, God wants our hearts. He wants *your* heart. And He's prepared to go to any length to express His love to you.

I believe, if you look, you will see His footprints right beside you. Through the driest deserts and darkest valleys, your heavenly Father loves and pursues you.

Throughout my recovery journey, I realized that there were some things I needed to forget. Some wounds, disappointments, and bitterness needed to get erased. However, God also helped me remember some of the greater things. His love is an anchor for stormy seas. And if there's anything we need in this world it's the eternal power, peace, and presence of the Almighty God.

No matter where you are today, I believe God has wonderful plans for your tomorrow. Remember, if you're breathing, God's not done with you yet. So maybe it's time for you to sit with Him and ask, "What's next?" Because I promise you, there is something amazing for you to step into.

Not easy. But Jesus never promised easy. He told the disciples in John 16:33, "I have told you these things, so that in me you may have peace. In this world you will have trouble. But take heart! I have overcome the world."

No matter our trouble, we have assurance.

No matter our anxiety, we have peace.

No matter how high the odds are stacked against us, we walk with an overcoming Jesus.

So take heart and step into your next with us.

*No matter where you are today,
I believe God has wonderful
plans for your tomorrow.*

Chapter 10

STEP INTO YOUR NEXT

*M*any days, I (Kristi) wish I could press a magic button and *reset everything back to "normal."* Our tragedy. Your heartbreak. The world's pain. And heck, while I'm at it, even Adam and Eve's fruit fiasco in the Garden! In the wake of tragedy, there's a profound sense that things weren't supposed to turn out the way they did.

Your friends from small group weren't supposed to get divorced ...

Your mother wasn't supposed to get cancer ...

Your child wasn't supposed to get in a car accident ...

Your company wasn't supposed to lay you off ...

Your house wasn't supposed to be destroyed by a natural disaster ...

Your church wasn't supposed to shut down after COVID ...

Your grandma wasn't supposed to suffer from dementia ...

Or most poignant for me, your husband wasn't supposed to have a cardiac arrest and nearly lose himself in the process ...

Before Scott collapsed on stage on that graduation Sunday in May 2020, we were moving a thousand miles an hour. Then, as fast as the pandemic shut the world down, our "normal" life evaporated. We were left with more questions than answers. And to me, decades full of prayers scribbled in notebooks and prophecies of massive ministry impact were about to go unanswered.

Then I remember what James 1:2-3 says, "Consider it pure joy, my brothers and sisters, whenever you face trials of many kinds, because you know that the testing of your faith produces perseverance."

Can I be real with y'all? Some days, those words are So. Dang. Annoying. Really, we're supposed to consider our pain "pure joy"? These last two years aren't even close to how Scott and I would have defined joy. But obviously James wasn't interested in our comfort as much as our ability to persevere. That's why he kept going in verse 4: "Let perseverance finish its work so that you may be mature and complete, not lacking anything."

Clearly, the path to spiritual maturity isn't comfort, it's crisis.

Is it just me, or does it seem like God doesn't care whether or not we want perseverance? He's never tended to ask, "Excuse me, Scott and Kristi, are you guys ready for some more perseverance? When would you like to get that scheduled?"

Instead, just like many of you, we got knocked out from a punch we never saw coming. However, do you know who isn't surprised by getting punched? Fighters. You know who's not surprised by getting shot at? Soldiers. You know who shouldn't be shocked they're under attack? Disciples of Jesus! And you know who is not surprised by the tragedy we were walking through? God.

None of this took Him by surprise. Neither does it surprise Him when you go through hard seasons. He's not up there thinking, "Oh wow, what just happened? I didn't know Scott had a cardiac arrest!" No, he stopped the Devil's attack to kill him, saying you cannot have him. And we are in the middle of what it looks like for God to use the Enemy's plans, meant for evil, for His glory and our good.

We're in a war that's been waged since before we were born. Every morning we wake up on the front lines of a battlefield. Paul put it this way: "For our struggle is not against flesh and blood, but against the rulers, against the authorities, against the powers of this dark world and against the spiritual forces of evil in the heavenly realms" (Ephesians 6:12).

So our doorsteps aren't just for welcome mats, they're war fronts. I *know* God has worked through our family. I *know* the calling that has directed Scott's life.

Clearly, the path to spiritual maturity isn't comfort, it's crisis.

And I *know* that the hit we took wasn't intended to knock us off balance, it was meant to take us out.

This became especially clear months into Scott's recovery. We sat on our living room couch on a rare night home in between our hodgepodge of treatments, therapies, and doctor appointments. My husband, a world-class pastor, speaker, leader, and daddy, sat slumped, almost buried into the cushions.

He said the most gut-wrenching words I've ever heard: "I wish I would have died. You kill a man before he dies when you take away his purpose."

I said, "Don't you ever say that again, Scott Schatzline." However, I understood his feelings.

It was the fall of 2020 now. For months, we'd been through the gauntlet of therapy. Still, Scott was only improving by inches when it seemed we had thousands of miles to go. He constantly struggled in the self-awareness that he couldn't do what he used to be able to do. However, our difficulty wasn't without its bright spots.[5]

WHAT DID SCOTT JUST SAY?!

We took Destiny to attend Bethel School of Supernatural Ministry in Redding, California in early September. This was Scott's first plane ride, and I definitely needed help, as he was getting more rascally by the day! So Pastor David came along with us. Have I said how we would not have made it without David and Cindy by our side? He and Scott were sitting together, and on a connecting flight, we were stuck on the tarmac for forty-five minutes. No one likes to sit in a stuffy tube with 200 irritated people they don't know while wearing masks. But this delay stretched Scott's patience thin and sent his temper into the stratosphere.

Before all of this, he would've been plenty patient and probably would have made friends with everyone sitting around him. That day, however, he was over the waiting game and threatening to start a mutiny.

---

[5]For example, Scott had spoken in tongues since being filled with the Holy Spirit as a child (it is also called a private prayer language or tongues of angels). Even though Scott was unable to speak or understand language after regaining consciousness, he could still speak in tongues–and used the *same words* and phrases he had long before the accident. God's gifts, and his spirit, were still very much alive in him. I count this as not only a bright spot, but a miracle showing God's power and the reality of this gift.

"This is not right," he kept repeating, "they need to give us our money back!"

He got progressively louder and louder, until he was nearly shouting. Pastor David was doing everything he could to calm him down. And then the crowning moment of the entire ordeal came when Scott noticed a man wearing a t-shirt that read: "Blue Lives Matter." That phrase was, of course, in support of our police forces across the country.

Something deep inside of Scott stirred, though. And after reading the statement, he began screaming (yes, *screaming*): "BLACK LIVES MATTER! BLACK LIVES MATTER!"

I don't think he could have yelled a more politically charged statement! It was both horrifying and hilarious at the same time. Of course, we appreciate our officers–but Scott has had a heart for racial reconciliation since he was a kid. It's part of our DNA at Daystar and even part and parcel for what it means to be a Schatzline.

While we have four biological children, we have a fifth child, Keithan Carroll, whom we functionally adopted in 1997. From day one, we loved Keithan like our very own. He had a voice in the family equal to everyone else's. He had a place at

our table with his name on it. And to this day, he is our son and we are his parents. But what has struck Keithan most about being so readily welcomed into the family is that he is African American. And in the deep South in the '90s, white families adopting black children was far from the norm. In fact, it caused friction with some people–which we were absolutely fine with. We saw Keithan as our son who happened to be African American. So, while a crazy political statement at the time, to Scott, myself, and our four biological children, black lives do matter, a whole lot.

But Scott's antics that day didn't stop there! We were eventually deplaned, and while en route to board our new flight, Scott started whispering: "Uh oh … Uh oh, David … Uh oh …"

David asked, "What's wrong, Pastor Scott?"

"I gotta tell her," he said, pointing ahead into a sea of people.

"You have to tell who?"

Pastor David followed Scott's finger to the woman he was pointing at. Now, I share this with all due respect, but the woman was obese, and Scott, being a health coach without a doggone filter, said, "She's fat. I have to tell her she's only got minutes left to live!"

Scott made a beeline for her, making Pastor David literally hold him back.

"You *can't* say stuff like that to people, Scott!"

At times, he was an endless stream of fun and hilarity. He got things stuck in his head that he compulsively let out (again, he had no filter). Just days after the airport incidents, Scott picked up the phrase, "Drop it like it's hot!"

Again, he had no idea what that actually meant, but repeated it over and over. One day, we stepped onto an elevator and were soon joined by a father and his young daughter, probably about seven years old. Scott was all smiles–and then we were joined by some new people on the next floor.

A man in a flamboyant suit and feather boa, joined by two *very* scantily clad women in string bikinis showing just about every inch of skin, stepped into the elevator. As if on cue, Scott looked at both of them and said, "Oh baby, drop it like it's hot!"

The ladies started saying, "Heyyyy!"

Now, he had zero sexual intention because he had no idea what the "it" was he told people to drop. But as the ladies laughed, and I covered my face with my hand in horror, Scott turned to the little girl and added, "Drop it like it's hot for Jesus!"

That really sent everyone over the top. So the risqué trio left, followed by the father and daughter, leaving Scott and I. He was still smiling and now telling me to drop it like it's hot, to which my only reply was, "Scott, you have *got* to stop saying that!"

THE UPS GIVE WAY TO THE DOWNS

When we arrived home, we started to host some close friends like Patrick and Christina Dopson who came to worship, encourage, and just spend time with us. Those moments would temporarily lift his spirits–but were short-lived.

They would leave and Scott's worsening depression would remain. Yet again, I felt helpless to do anything except research, call doctors, and be with him every waking moment. We needed a breakthrough–and even at this stage, though it seemed far away, I knew there had to be some stone we had yet to overturn.

Then, one morning in September I got a call from a dear friend, Dan, in our coaching network. Real hope blossomed.

"Kristi, I want to connect you with friends of mine, Doctors Robert and Jeralyn Brossfield. We are spending some time together in Colorado right now and I explained Scott's story to them. They are doing groundbreaking work for people with traumatic brain injuries. And their technology is healing their patients' brains in ways the medical world has never seen before," Dan said.

"Yes, absolutely yes!" I said. "What is it? Where is it? How does it work?"

I wanted to know everything.

"Basically, they would hook Scott up to a machine, measure his brainwave activity, and map out a treatment plan to get the different parts of his brain to talk again. They help a lot of soldiers repair brain damage and recover from PTSD no one else was able to fix."

"So it could *change his brain*?" I asked.

"I think so," he said. "I'll connect you."

I tried to keep my expectations in check. I was sick of having our glimmers of hope choked out by stormy clouds of disappointment. Still, something about this seemed different. At this stage, I knew if we wanted answers and real healing, we would find it on a path we hadn't yet walked.

HOPE

Scott had suffered an anoxic brain injury when he lost consciousness during his cardiac arrest. This happens when your brain is deprived of oxygen for more than four minutes. After that, brain cells get wiped out by the millions. Then, at five minutes, the damage becomes *permanent*.

Typical symptoms include:[6]

- Short-term memory loss,
- Poor executive function (like judgment, reason, processing information, etc.),
- Aphasia (difficulty using words or processing their meaning),
- Trouble processing visual information,
- Ataxia (lack of physical coordination like wobbly walking),
- Apraxia (inability to do common tasks),
- Dysarthria (difficulty speaking due to an inability to control the muscles used in speech),
- And so much more . . .

---

[6]Anoxic brain injury - brainandspinalcord.org: Brain & Head Injury trauma. Brain and Spinal Cord. (2019, October 9). Retrieved April 25, 2022, from https://www.brainandspinalcord.org/anoxic-brain-injury/

Scott had every one of these complications on steroids. It wasn't just that he couldn't remember new pieces of information—it's that most of his memory had been wiped out. In the realm of anoxic brain injury there was a scale of severity: mild, moderate, severe—and Scott.

Scott's brain was without oxygen for 22 minutes.

It was a miracle his brain survived the massive cellular death at all. But some days we wondered if this was it. So when we connected with Dr. Brossfield and the Brain Treatment Center,[7] we found hope—though still mixed with doubt. Their technology, called Magnetic e-Resonance Therapy (mERT), had a real chance to heal Scott. We would have to travel for long periods to Palm Springs, California. But at this stage, we would've gone to Antarctica if there was a chance to make Scott better!

The most wonderful thing is that we had actually met them at a national conference for our coaching business—and they remembered meeting us! Not only were they brilliant doctors and cutting-edge researchers, they were the most caring, tender-hearted people we'd ever met. Beyond their capability to help Scott, we knew they cared deeply about him as a person. This was the first time we'd felt this kind of care, concern, and confidence. Our first conversation lasted for an hour (rather than the usual eight to ten minutes). And even more crazy, these doctors let us talk, unload, and explain exactly what had happened. They genuinely listened and stepped into our pain with us—so much so we cried together.

On the other hand, the final day we visited his last treatment center, that doctor left us with this prognosis: "The way Scott is now, is your new normal. I'd advise you to get used to it."

We've always wanted to know the truth. But the cold indifference and unconcern made the news that much more crushing. The Brossfields didn't accept that story. We knew we'd found champions who wouldn't give up on us and move

---

[7]https://braintreatmentcenter.com

on to the next case like we were just numbers on a spreadsheet, another patient to tally against their bottom line.

It would be a significant investment, but the Brossfields' generosity coupled with *unbelievable* financial support from family, friends locally, and our coaching community (that we never even asked for!) made it possible for us to move forward. We didn't know what it would look like, but we were hopeful it would help. So we packed up and flew to California to begin Scott's treatment. However, the first step was a rude awakening.

20/200

"Scott, answer the questions on this iPad," a nurse said, handing the tablet to Scott.

He looked at the screen in utter confusion. I could tell he wasn't even sure what he was looking at, much less how to follow the instructions. I wanted to help Scott with every question, spatial-reasoning puzzle, and image, but this was a test of his mind, not mine. So he had to muddle through on his own, confused and frustrated. And as he tapped the screen, the computer tallied Scott's cognitive abilities on a sliding scale of 0 to 200 (with 200 being a perfect score).

Scott scored 20/200.

I had to find gratitude here to keep the disappointment from overwhelming me. Parts of his brain were unharmed, meaning he could still walk, use his hands, and talk. Continued improvement was a real potential. However, the neurons in his frontal and central brain weren't firing. They were supposed to have nice peaks to show proper activity, but they were flatlined.

Imagine your brain as a series of freeways in a large city. They connect traffic from the suburbs to downtown to wherever else millions of people need to go. When the roads are stable, traffic flows as intended. Now imagine if two-thirds of the freeway bridges were removed. So traffic ran into a dead end with an insurmountable gap.

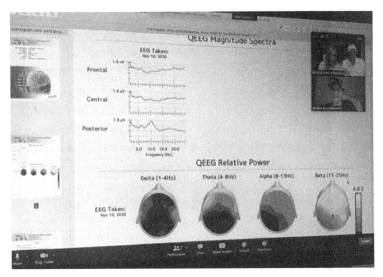

This image is a scan of Scott's brain taken on November 10, 2020
at the beginning of his treatment. The posterior frequency is healthy,
but the frontal and central frequency lines are flat, which showed
exactly where he needed rehabilitation.

That's what happened to Scott's brain. The flow of communication was cut off. They had no way to connect and coordinate. However, this was precisely where his treatment would begin. His rehabilitation would focus on finding detours to reconnect the flow of "traffic," and train his brain to talk to itself again.

Shortly after his treatments began, I received a call from our dear friend, Philip Cameron. He's an evangelist, author, and singer whose ministry has touched millions of lives especially in the country of Moldova.[8] It was exactly the call I needed. Though we spoke about many things, I'll never forget the message he had for me.

"Kristi, you are doing all of the right things. Paint the blood of Calvary over Scott's mind every day. I believe he will be healed."

He had no idea what was happening with Scott's brain at the exact moment we spoke. But his encouragement was the

---

[8]You can learn more about his ministry here: philipdcameron.com

perfect example of Proverbs 25:11 (NLV): "A word spoken at the right time is like fruit of gold set in silver."

We have learned that when you're leaders, everyone assumes people are speaking life into you. They think you automatically understand that you're appreciated, doing things right, and are making a difference. However, I can tell you that I take every opportunity to encourage the leaders in my life, because they are often the most under-encouraged people. They pour into everyone else but can be left with empty tanks. So Pastor Cameron's word was like rain in the desert of my soul. He gave me strength to keep fighting for Scott when I desperately needed it, because we still had a long way to go.

THANK GOD FOR PROGRESS

We fell into a rhythm during those six weeks of treatment. We'd wake up, bask in morning sunlight, worship and pray, feed the ducks in a serene little pond behind our hotel, and then head to the clinic. The treatment itself was unlike anything we'd encountered so far.

A machine with a reticulating arm moved a set of magnets around Scott's head. At each location it erupted in a rapid series of clicking noises and Scott would need to close his eyes. His face twitched and contracted as electrical impulses fired through his forehead, face, and into his jaw muscles. It was painful at the front of his skull where the complex layers of facial muscles danced involuntarily at the charges coursing through. With each treatment, though, we saw progress. Real, honest-to-God progress.

We both knew things were looking up in the first week. One morning while we were getting ready to head to the clinic, I walked out of the bathroom in our hotel room and saw Scott doing something absolutely shocking: he was ironing!

Literally, a day before he couldn't even put words to what an iron or iron board were—much less use one. And now, not only did he know what it was, he'd picked out his own shirt, realized it was wrinkled, and ironed it (better than I could have, by the way). This was my Scott–Mr. Sharp Dresser himself–coming back!

His psychologist was blown away as well, explaining that he was starting to skyrocket on the recovery curve.

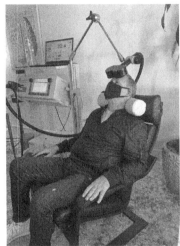

OASIS IN THE WILDERNESS

My (Scott's) depression finally started to lift when I could see improvements for myself. And I remember Kristi saying, "Baby, we finally have the numbers. Factually, scientifically, without a doubt, you are improving."

We returned for a second round of mERT treatment in March 2021, where I made even more progress. When I wasn't being treated, one of our favorite places to explore and keep active was Tahquitz Canyon, also known as the Indian Canyons. They are breathtaking and were the home of the Agua Caliente Band of Cahuilla Indians. These canyons look straight out of a fantasy movie. Palm trees grow between giant canyon walls. There's so much life bursting in the middle of the desert–it's a literal oasis.

Hiking the canyons is a profound experience. As you're walking, you can look back and see the path you've been on.

However, you can't see what lies ahead beyond the next bend. You must take one step at a time, trusting in the signs as you move forward on your journey. There's no way to predict what comes next; all you know is that another wonderful turn of adventure is ahead.

A cross stood high atop one of the canyons. It felt so far away, but we kept hiking toward it. I knew I was tired physically and wanted to quit, but if I could push through the pain and keep my eyes on the cross that I could make it. This reminded me of an old gospel song, "If I could find my way back to the cross, I could find my way back home." And as we focused on it, it grew larger, and the distance grew smaller. We're always learning and *re-learning* to keep our focus on the cross, the finished work of Jesus for us!

This reminded me of Psalm 119:105, where David says, "Your word is a lamp for my feet, a light on my path." That's how we've felt throughout this entire experience. We have barely had enough light to see our next step. But we never stopped walking. When we thought we found the end of our path, God revealed where to go next. Every footfall is a choice to embrace faith over fear.

> We're always learning and *re-learning* to keep our focus on the cross, the finished work of Jesus for us!

My friends, don't be scared of your path. In those canyons I boldly began to declare, "If I can, you can." I know if we could make it through all of this, God is going to lead you through your wilderness as well. Trust the path. Follow the signposts. Hold onto his promises and Word.

You *will* step into your next.

TIME TO MOVE FORWARD

I (Kristi) have watched Scott heal. I've heard him prophesy things to people that were completely beyond his ability to comprehend when he shared them. I've seen him grow by leaps and bounds as his mind has returned. However, the journey has been through a winter that just won't go away. Many times I would say his recovery reminds me of what it's like for a town to recover after an F5 tornado destroys everything in its path. It may take many years to rebuild. Years where tarps cover houses and parcels of land lay wiped clean. But don't despair, because what is rebuilt can be even more beautiful than before. It will just take time to get there.

We catch glimpses of spring. Feel the sun on our skin. See buds on the trees. Smell the flowers and start to blossom. And then we're hit with mornings of icy frost, curling the still-budding leaves to brown. Fog rolls in, crowding out the sunlight. And a damp cold that sinks into our bones sets in.

This journey has required constant faith.

Not coffee mug faith.

Not greeting card sayings.

Not cute wall hangings with hand-lettered Bible verses.

Every moment of every hour of every day reminds us that our old life—a life we loved and had found our stride within—was taken from us. It's gone. We are left with the constant question, "What happens now, God?"

Our purpose used to be so clear. We had our place, people, and plan. Then our ship smashed into rocks we couldn't see, punching a hole in the hull of our dreams, and we started sinking fast. We had to tread water alone on an angry sea. But even in the waves I believe God doesn't teach us to swim only to let us drown. He didn't bring us this far to *only bring us this far*. Neither did he bring Scott back from the dead to leave him this way.

The pain is still present—but so is God's hand. So are our people. Our amazing kids encouraging and caring for us (all while having grandbabies, graduating from school, and moving across the country). Our incredible church staff who have stood in the leadership gap. Our wonderful Daystar Church family supporting us. And our health coaching community overwhelming us with support.

While we've seen progress, we still have a long journey ahead. As we write this book together, Scott's cognitive abilities are still not at the standards we had hoped they would be. But I promise you, our story is one of *hope*. It's about God's *good plans* amidst *terrible circumstances*.

Don't feel sad for us. And don't stay in sorrow for any situation you are in. If anything, we have learned perspective. Life in God's family isn't about denying our pain or minimizing tragedy, it's about zooming out and seeing the big picture: what the Enemy means for evil our God turns for good. Even though we may not see any possibility of redemption, we trust His promise in Isaiah 55:8-9:

> "'For my thoughts are not your thoughts,
> neither are your ways my ways,'
> declares the Lord.
> 'As the heavens are higher than the Earth,
> so are my ways higher than your ways
> and my thoughts than your thoughts.'"

We may never know why we have walked this painful road on this side of eternity. But He does. Most days, fully trusting God is all we have. Faith has become more than a throwaway buzzword—we *know* what trusting God in the face of doubt and fear means.

After finishing Scott's brain treatments, believe it or not, I fell into the darkest depression of my life. Though I never let Scott see me crying, I wept bitterly. I never said the words out loud, but I have still had moments where I've felt like walking away (though I never would have). I've still pleaded with God in the dead of night, "When are you going to give us a miracle?"

He said, "I could give you a miracle right now, but it will stop the greater future I have planned for you."

And that's the crux: do I believe Him?

That's the question for you, too. Do you believe God? Do you believe He is who He says? That He will do what He's promised?

If Scott and I could sum up what we've learned in a single word, it would be this: *believe*. Belief in God's goodness, nearness, and faithfulness is the most powerful way to punch back when the Devil tries to knock you down. When life overwhelms you, believe.

Punching back means turning your *test* into a *test-imony!*

If Scott and I could sum up what we've learned in a single word, it would be this: believe.

We sing about our trust in God's faithfulness every Sunday. But do we really believe what we're saying? You'll find out in the testing. You'll learn the substance and size of your faith in the dark valleys. To paraphrase A.W. Tozer: "We Christians don't tell lies, we sing them on Sunday mornings."

I'm not saying this on a high horse. I'm sharing it as a lesson from the trenches. Because if you would have asked me on May 16, 2020 (the day before Scott's first incident) what the next season was going to look like, I would've told you about our giant plans, strategies, and goals. In our ministry, in our business, in our family. We were going to conquer the world and outshine the pandemic.

We had no idea what was ahead. Neither do you. And that's okay. We don't know what tomorrow will bring. But we know who holds every tomorrow.

This journey has stripped away the ugly and gross things in us. It has humbled me. It has challenged me to stop making myself the center of the universe. It has also strengthened me, providing a confidence and security in who God created me to be. I'm so thankful for Pastor Al Brice, reminding us of Job 14:7: "For there is hope for a tree, if it is cut down, that it will sprout again." These kinds of words strengthened us enough to keep moving forward.

Friends, we live in a hard world that isn't fair. We can ask all we want, "Why did this happen to me when other peoples' lives are so much easier?"

While those thoughts will come, they will not serve you. Giving root to them sprouts weeds of giving up when God has seeds of hope to blossom in your life. Scott and I want our lives to reflect remarkable faith. The kind of faith that makes people ask, "How on Earth can they still be walking?"

We know who we are in Christ. We believe we are more than conquerors. And we know what God does for people who daily take up their crosses and follow Him. We have learned to cultivate a culture of honor. Honoring God and His plans first.

No matter where you are, don't quit moving forward. Don't stop believing. The glory of what's ahead will be greater than what you have left behind. Don't stay face down on the mat. Get up and punch back with *belief*. We serve a God who creates life where there was only death. I know this firsthand, because I'm married to a miracle man whose smile, kindness, and love remind me every day that God's not done with us yet.

As Scott says, if you're still breathing, He's not done with you, either.

ACKNOWLEDGMENTS

*W*e *could have never made it through this season without the love and support of our family, our community, and so many others that have been on this journey with us!* Our hearts is full of gratitude beyond our expression and we want to try our best to acknowledge everyone.

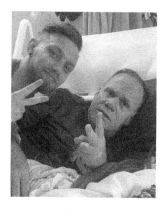

To Ethan, Ale and Camila, Easy E, E-man, you were the first to make us parents and we have always been so proud of you. There's an unexplainable, incomprehensible love you experience when you become a parent and I know you and Ale understand that now that you have your precious Camila. There isn't anything a parent wouldn't do for their child and now you have shown that same love to us, your parents. You have been there for us, traveled thousands of miles, jumped on planes, spent the night with your dad, took care of him, honored him, gave us wisdom, sat on the couch and let me cry on your shoulder, and been a great big brother to all of your siblings. When I just wanted to ramble I knew I could call either one of you. Thank you for being levelheaded and courageous, and bringing a sense of calm into our anxiety. Thank you Ale, you always give me space to share my heart and make me feel so loved. Thank you for being the amazing son and daughter-in-love that you are.

To Noah, Emily and Elowyn, our hearts are so full of joy to see the difficulties you have overcome because we know that you are destined for greatness. Noah the King, and sometimes Bishop, you stood through the darkest moments and fought through every battle that came our way even while you were fighting your own. You and Emily made our struggle a little lighter by bringing Elowyn into our world. Her beautiful smile and the way she always wants Grandaddy to hold her makes our hearts happy. You've been right here with us from the very first medical scare, showing such courage and strength, staying in the hospital with your dad, caring for him in ways that brought honor and respect. Thank you both for never letting us give up or stop believing that we were going to make it through this. Emily, you've been a late night shoulder to cry on, and you always made it easy to talk when I couldn't even put my thoughts into words. Noah, thank you for being strong and rising up in the middle of the pain you were feeling, being such a man of God and caring for your dad the way you have. We couldn't have made it without you. We love you and Emily with all our hearts!

To Keithan, Danielle, Nehemiah, Xander, and Elijah, we had no idea the blessing that was coming our way twenty-four years ago when Keithan became our son at sixteen years old. We are so proud of the man of God, husband and daddy you have become as well as the professional CEO business owner you've become. You stayed strong through this journey, and you're the best big brother and leader to your siblings. You and Danielle gave us three beautiful and smart little boys, Nehemiah, Xander, and Elijah. They bring us such joy! You never hesitated to travel even while Danielle was pregnant with twins. Never once did you complain, you just did it. If you knew I needed you, there was no question, you were here. Thank you for always making a phone call when we needed to hear encouragement, wisdom for the next steps we needed to take, and strength and determination when we wanted to quit. Danielle, you've put together this entire book launch, worked in the middle of toddlers running around like wild boys, and always kept your cool. You're so encouraging and confidently push us toward our destiny, always believing in our "crazy faith," making the most amazing social media posts, supporting us in every idea, and showing us how to make it happen. We are beyond grateful for you both and your love for us. We love you more than you know.

To Isaiah and Kelsie, our little Zay Zay, Mom and Dad are so grateful for you and Kelsie. From Kentucky, Alabama, California and now North Carolina, it didn't matter where you were geographically, you were always with us. You not only fought with us in the spirit but you showed up and spent time in the hospital, reading the Bible to your dad, encouraging him, and believing for his full recovery to manifest. You've brought such sweetness to our lives, such joy and courage, such strength. Thank you for being a prophetic voice in our lives during this season. Thank you for giving as much time as we needed on a call or a FaceTime just to talk through our pain, confusion, questions, crazy thoughts, and even the what if's. It never failed; after a phone call with you, we felt empowered and strengthened, and believed in our dreams again. You and Kelsie make us so proud to watch how God is using you for His glory and how God taught you about the importance of honor and vulnerability. Thank you for sharing your wisdom and becoming our teacher. You have only tipped the iceberg for all that God has for you!

To Destiny, we always knew our strong-willed, determined, steadfast, won't take no for an answer, daddy's little girl would use those character traits one day for Jesus and for good, but we didn't know you would stare death in the face and declare your dad to live and not die. You've walked this journey right beside us with courage, strength, power, wisdom, and so much love. You stood beside me the night your dad left us for a short time and became my strength when I was in total shock. It was supposed to be your season to celebrate graduating high school and going off to college, but you never once complained. You actually carried me (Mom) and put your own hurt and pain to the side. I know you felt lost and alone, and I wish you never had to experience this, but you are one strong and powerful young woman of God because of the fire you have walked through. Thank you for always FaceTiming us at least three times a day while you were away at Bethel. Thank you for caring for your daddy with such patience and love, traveling with us, watching after him, being super protective, and always being able to talk him into doing the right thing when he was done listening to me. It never fails; all I have to say is, "Let's call Destiny and see what she has to say," and he would always listen. We love you, Destiny Moriah-Grace Schatzline! You will change the world.

To "Dee" Dacquistoe Hamner, we have a special bond; spiritual son doesn't cover our whole relationship. You were brought into our lives as a son, a part of our biological family, as a brother to our children, God-chosen. You have a special place in our hearts, you have been beside us through this roller coaster of life, always available to chat, and never failing to speak life and positive words to us. We love you Dee! We are so thankful God gave us you.

To my (Scott's) brother Pat and sister-in-love Karen, you may be older, but I'm the better looking of the two. Pat, your wisdom, love and support, right-time moments of prophetic words, calls, texts, and posts all at the right time during this journey gave us the very push sometimes to make it to the next day. Pat, you would always FaceTime with Scott when he was confused and couldn't understand who he was, where he was, or what was happening. You walked him through so many dark nights even on sunny days. We love you and Karen with all our hearts.

To (Scott's) Dad, also known as Papa, Bishop, or Daddy, you didn't even have time to grieve losing the love of your life just two weeks before when you had to shift all your energy to fighting for me in prayer. I'm forever grateful that you put aside yourself and stepped up to help bring stability and strength to the church so I could recover and regain myself. We love you, Dad, you are the best!

To (Kristi's) Mom and Dad, Judy and Jerry, thank you for every phone call, hug, encouraging word, and all the laughter you bring. A merry heart is good like medicine and you always gave us something to laugh about. You've been right beside us every step of the way. I love you more today than I ever thought I could. Thank you for not just being my mama, but being my best friend.

To my (Kristi's) sister Wanda Cole and brother Scott Kizziah, you have always been right by my side with a listening ear and a shoulder to cry on. I love you so much!

To David and Cindy Redding, it's so hard to even put into words how grateful we are for both of you. You went far above and beyond the call of duty. You both were always right there with us, walking through every scary moment, staring death in the face, but fighting with power and faith. You kept me (Kristi) from losing my cool, especially with the nurse that kept calling me "sweetie," and kept Scott from getting in trouble on the plane and in the airport (haha). You traveled with us, protected Scott, spent hours in the hospital room, ICU, and rehab, and kept the church running strong in the middle of it all. Cindy, thank you for always being Scott's biggest cheerleader and always giving him whatever he asked for. You guys never left our side and we are forever grateful. Thank you for your loyalty and commitment to us through this journey.

To Dr. Brent and Cherelle Tidwell, God knew when he put us together six years ago. We thought it was to merge our churches, but little did we know that God had a plan for you, Dr. Brent, to be one of the first chosen as a part for Scott's chance to survive. We are eternally grateful that you did not stop, you did not let your arms get tired, and even if they did, you weren't quitting. Cherelle, thank you for always speaking life to us and finding the sunshine in the middle of a massive storm. We love you both with all our heart.

To Russ and Traci Scarce, I don't know what we would have done if Traci hadn't listened to the Holy Spirit to call me and without a second thought Russ hadn't jumped on a plane and come all the way to Alabama from California to stay with Scott at night for a week while he was still in ICU. I knew he would be OK in your care and that you would protect him. Thank you for allowing me to have some peaceful nights of sleep. Thank you for sitting up with Scott every night watching over him while he tried to sleep. Sometimes family doesn't always mean blood relatives.

To Wayne and Courtney Pendle, God knew we needed you both in our lives and he brought us together because we all said yes to our health and went to Costa Rica together! We had no idea all the life we would do together after that trip. Thank you for always being there for us, laughing with us, making us laugh so hard our faces hurt, and speaking wisdom and truth even when it didn't feel good. Thank you for all the late night calls, texts, morning coffee dates, spur-of-the-moment getaways, and sleepovers with all the "sleep sounds" and "face cream." We have walked through so much together; it's rare to find best friends like you. We couldn't imagine having to go through this life without having you by our sides. Thank you for being our friends.

To Pastor Al and Tava Brice, there are no words to truly describe how you both have impacted our lives. The one thing we know now more than ever before is the love of God and how it is the most important thing you can carry with you in life. Thank you for showing us this. Thank you for loving us unconditionally. Thank you for believing in us even when it seemed impossible. Thank you for being faith for us when we didn't have very much. Thank you for loving us like your own children. Thank you for speaking life and empowering us to go forward and trust God. Thank you for being the example to breaking off religion and thank you for trusting us to lead the house in worship at Covenant Love back in 1998. We would not be who we are today if you both had not been part of our lives. We love you!

To Doug and Thea Wood, this book is actually a reality because you believed it needed to get out. Doug, you told me, "Get this story out now." I was scared, afraid, and feared failing. Thea, thank you for empowering us to "Kick Fear in the Face" and push through the storms. Without your belief in us, we would never have stepped out in faith the way we did to put this story on paper and now into the lives of many who will find strength and hope. God brought you into our lives for such a time as this.

To Harry and Cheryl Salem (Miss America 1980), if we ever felt like we needed someone in our corner to help us fight the fight of faith, we knew we could call you. Thank you for always taking our pain and showing us how to turn it into a promise. You've persevered through so many battles and been a Godly example of standing strong in the midst of the storm.

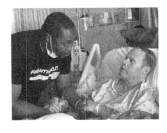

To Julian Cheese, you've always been right there with us, from giving us rides to the hospital, answering every question we had about medical concerns, or calling your doctor friends to get an answer for us, to staying in the hospital and singing the old songs "Smile" and "The Reason Why I Sing." You always, always stayed positive and even called the kids to speak life and love over them. You've been on Pop Scott's pants leg since you were a little boy and grew up to be one anointed worship leader. You make us so proud in so many ways.

To Eddie Murphy, I want to thank you so much for being there for me (Scott), for showing up in the hospital to give me a clean cut and shave and helping me to look good in the hospital. You always took care of me, showed up at our house, played games with me, and protected me. Thank you for making me feel like I'm still a pastor. You influence so many lives, not just

as a barber, but as a daddy and a pastor to so many. You make me so proud, and it's such an honor to do life with you and Kisha. We love you!

To Frank Carnaggio Photography and Melissa Bogardus, a huge thank you to the greatest photographer, hair and make-up artist, and photo shoot designer! You took two simple people that just wanted a couple photos and did what you do. We couldn't be prouder of the images you captured while making us feel like superstars. You have worked all around the world, but you took time to share this journey with us. Thank you!

To Shannon Allen, words simply cannot express how we feel about you. We love you so much! You have always been our biggest cheerleader in every ministry idea, event to be planned, and thought we whispered. You took each idea and ran with it. Thank you for seeing the positive in everything we have walked through and inspiring us with wisdom, creativity, and the Word, always.

To Patrick and Christina Dopson, first, we are so proud of everything you are accomplishing and how you are impacting the world in ways you never realized. Christina, you are a powerful woman of wisdom, an amazing wife, and mother. But personally, to us, you are the most encouraging, life-giving voice of strength in our darkest moments. Thank you for always supporting us, having a God word for us, coming to see us, taking the time to listen, and letting us cry on your shoulder. We truly are grateful that God put us together over thirty years ago.

To Paul Arthurs, Tochi Agomo, Lynn Russ, and Tim Cravens, you dropped everything and traveled many miles to stay with Scott in the hospital to give me a moment of rest. Tochi, you came to our house every single Thursday to take our trash out, and again on Friday to put the trash cans back in place. Mrs. Lynn gave the best leg and foot massages, played games, took Scott on walks, worked on his at-home therapy, took us to doctor appointments, took us for Scott's defibrillator implant surgery, carried us back when the bleeding wouldn't stop, and the list goes on and on and on. We love you all so much!

To Dr. Wayne Scott Andersen, you have shown thousands, actually millions, the way to live a healthy lifestyle, and you found time for us personally. Our family history has been set on a new course because of you. Dr. A, I am so grateful for you and the time you took to call me during the most critical moments of Scott's life. You walked me through the questions and medical terms that I did not understand. You called us family and were with us on the frontline of the battle. We are forever grateful for the love you showed to us.

To all the EMTs, doctors, nurses, therapists, and the greater medical team, we are so grateful for all of you and your years of study and sacrifice to serve our community. Thank you for never giving up on Scott, always searching for an answer, and giving us hope that he was going to survive. Even though we were told the facts, we felt so blessed to have been surrounded by so many that believed with us for Scott's miracle.

I also want to highlight a few names that have walked this out with us from the beginning and gave us the hope we needed to never give up. Without you, Scott's recovery would not have been possible: Dr. Bryan King, Dr. Donald Gross, Dr. Crystal Skinner, Dr. Morgan Goss, Dr. Sakina Kamal, Dr. Craig Buettner, Dr. Jamie Lowther, Jamie Calaway, Charlotte Rogers, Tricia Murphy, Jessica Gray Lee, Katie Reid, Dr. Carson Byrd, Dr. Dinesh Chandra, Cody, Jessi Cowan, Kristina Gregory, Heather Batey, Drs. Jeralyn & Robert Brossfield, and the Brain Treatment Team.

To Scott Herndon and the Carroll's Creek Volunteer Fire Dept. team, words can never truly express the gratitude in my heart for how you and your team showed up and gave Scott a chance to survive. It was Father's Day, you were with your family, and you chose to serve us that day. Thank you for your service to our community. Thank you most of all for stopping, after the ambulance left with Scott, to pray for all of our family that night. You will never know how many lives you have touched. We are forever grateful!

To our family, friends, and many spiritual sons and daughters, the term spiritual sons and daughters can have a negative impression in the world but it shouldn't. God has always blessed us with family that even though they are not blood-related, they are held close to our heart. You have all walked this journey with us, and many times when we were struggling the most with deep pain, fear, and even depression, you would call, text, and sometimes show up on our doorstep, leave us groceries ordered from Instacart, or send a DoorDash meal. Really just knowing you were there gave us comfort. We are so very thankful to have been blessed by God with the best family and friends.

To Jordan Loftis and the Story Chorus team, thank you for the hours upon hours you've spent bringing this story to the page and to the lives of so many. You helped us say things we didn't know how to put into words. You let us cry and be scared and relive every hellish moment, but you always gave us time to find the light in the middle of the darkness. You fully invested in our journey; never once did you make us feel like our thoughts or ideas were ill-conceived or unwise. You cheered us on, helped us think things through, and showed us how our own experiences could be a beautiful testimony to give someone else hope in their storm. Thank you for your patience, your brilliance, and your creativity! We are forever grateful for this journey with you. It's brought us both so much healing and strength to move forward. We love all of you!

To our Daystar pastors, directors, staff, leaders, and elders, we have been together for so many years and you've always run alongside us. Never could we do the work that God has called us to do without you. You all stood beside us, called us, loved on us, encouraged us, believed in us, and continued carrying the torch when your leader was down and needed to reset. We pray that you receive hundredfold in return for the days and nights you've sown into our lives and the lives of countless others. We love each and every one of you with all our hearts: Bishop Pat Schatzline, David & Cindy Redding, Kim & Wayne Holyfield, Charles & Betty Standford, Howard & Cecy Bosman, Noah Schatzline, Dalton & Jenna Ballew, DeShawn & Raytonya Hughes, Shi & Mokonde Hales, Karen Harless, Chris Palmore, Alice & Pop Redding, Esther Jimenez, Cristian Zavala, Jeff Harless, Danyelle Lavender, Eddie & Keisha Murphy, Julian & Amanda Cheese, Billy & Anjanette Hicks, Acie & Tracie Thomas, Dexter & Mildred Robertson, Bryan and Reneé Allen, Joseph & Chandra O'Bryant, Clay & Laura Clark, Shannon Allen, Gloria & Willie Foster, Ed & Veronica Giles, Ben & Julie Rodriguez, Andrew & Nimi Ighofose, Myron & LeAnn Shiers, Laverne & Kelvin Schatzline, Johnnie & Nichole Redding, Greg & Tamar Wilson, Jose & Nancy de la Torre, Gabby Pettway, Jeff & Kristie Eiland, Kerrington Kennedy, Cynthia Washington, Charles Clark, Terry & Maurice Turner, Chris & Ella Stewart, Fred & Dorinda Trick, Jerome & Robben Hewitt, Danny & Tina Dubose, Paul & Elaine Smith, Brent & Cherelle Tidwell, Lynn & Mixon Russ.

To our Daystar church family, we fought this battle together. Thank you for your prayers, intercession, meals, baskets of goodies, cards, texts, phone calls, encouragement, and for never giving up. We have been in a war and you walked into the battlefield with us and God could not be more proud of this family for standing and fighting together. We love each and every one of you with all our hearts!

To our Optavia community, our lives took a turn for the better about six years ago when God put this amazing plan in our lives. We thought it would just help us lose weight, but it changed our mindset and gave us a new outlook on life. What we didn't know it was going to give us was the close friendships that would develop and have now impacted us personally for our greater good. When Scott went down, we were flooded with all of your calls, texts, love, and support. We love all of you with a love that can't be explained.

To all of you who supported us and chipped in on the expense for Scott's brain treatment and recovery process, we were totally overwhelmed by your love, support, random cash apps, cards in the mail, Marriott points, and the list goes on and on. Without your support, Scott would not have been able to make the trip and begin the tremendous healing process that has now given him the opportunity to be Scott again. And you helped give me back my sweetheart. We could never repay all of you for your generosity and your love. Thank you!

ABOUT SCOTT AND KRISTI

*S*cott *and Kristi Schatzline live to see others walk in the full potential of who they are created to be!* They are passionate pursuers of Christ, and they love people unconditionally. They lead a beautiful, multicultural congregation at Daystar Family Church in Northport, Alabama, where experiencing and sharing God's love is the number one priority. Both as pastors and health coaches, they have inspired thousands to live their best life and walk in full health: spirit, soul, and body.

Scott and Kristi married in 1991 and served as worship pastors for Scott's father at Daystar for seven years. In 1998, Scott and Kristi were called to serve as worship pastors for Covenant Love Church with Pastors Al and Tava Brice in Fayetteville, North Carolina. In the summer of 2004, they heard the Macedonia call to return home to Daystar. From the beginning, Daystar Family Church focused on the love of God and the power of unity. The desire is to be a church that looks like heaven with all nations and a place of freedom for everyone.

On Father's Day 2020, Scott experienced what is known as a sudden-death cardiac arrest. After several minutes, the paramedics were able to revive and stabilize him. Due to the prolonged time period that his brain was deprived of oxygen, Scott experienced memory loss as well as many other symptoms. Scott is a fighter and he has valiantly pursued health and wholeness on this journey. He has relearned basic things like walking, talking, and everyday tasks. He is progressing in recapturing his memories and his cognitive abilities.

Throughout this journey that they are walking, they have motivated so many to keep fighting and pushing forward. Scott and Kristi stand on the promise that the supernatural love of God is what draws people to the Lord and brings healing, hope, and freedom.

Scott and Kristi live in Tuscaloosa, Alabama and they have five beautiful children: Ethan (Alejandra), Noah (Emily), Keithan (Danielle), Isaiah (Kelsie), and Destiny, as well as their grandchildren Nehemiah, Elijah, Xander, Elowyn, and Camila.

Made in the USA
Monee, IL
17 October 2022

16082851R00103